CAVENDISH PRA

Private Company Law

THIRD EDITION

MARK STAMP
PARTNER, LINKLATERS

SERIES EDITOR
CM BRAND, SOLICITOR

Cavendish
Publishing
Limited

London • Sydney

Third edition first published in Great Britain 2001 by Cavendish Publishing Limited, The Glass House, Wharton Street, London WC1X 9PX

Telephone: +44 (0)20 7278 8000   Facsimile: +44 (0)20 7278 8080
Email: info@cavendishpublishing.com
Website: www.cavendishpublishing.com

© Stamp, M   2001
Second edition 1996
Third edition   2001

All rights reserved. No part of this publication may be reproduced, stored in a retrieval system, or transmitted, in any form or by any means, electronic, mechanical, photocopying, recording, scanning or otherwise, except under the terms of the Copyright Designs and Patents Act 1988 or under the terms of a licence issued by the Copyright Licensing Agency, 90 Tottenham Court Road, London W1P 9HE, UK, without the permission in writing of the publisher.

Stamp, MA
Private company law – 3rd ed – (Practice notes series)
1 Private companies – Great Britain 2 Corporation law – Great Britain
I Title II Brand, Clive, M
346.4'1'0668

ISBN 1 85941 457 5
Printed and bound in Great Britain

Acknowledgments

I would like to thank Matthew Elliot and Emma Beddington for their valuable help and assistance in bringing this third edition to fruition.

Contents

1 Sources and Definitions   **1**

    1.1   Source material   1

    1.2   Definitions   2

2 Introduction   **11**

    2.1   What is a private company?   11

    2.2   Types of private companies   13

    2.3   The consequences of incorporation   14

    2.4   Protection of creditors   14

    2.5   Statute   16

    2.6   Case law   16

3 Formation   **19**

    3.1   Matters to be considered prior to forming a company   19

    3.2   Formation of a company   23

    3.3   Company notepaper   24

    3.4   Publicity of name   25

    3.5   Company books   25

    3.6   Matters to be dealt with at first board meeting   27

    3.7   First general meeting of the company   27

4 The Companies Register — 29

4.1	Company searches	29
4.2	Who to ask at Companies House	31
4.3	Matters required to be registered	31
4.4	Constructive notice	32
4.5	Compliance	33

5 The Memorandum of Association and the Doctrine of *Ultra Vires* — 35

5.1	The contents of the memorandum	35
5.2	The objects clause	35
5.3	The doctrine of *ultra vires*	37
5.4	Dealings by a third party with officers of the company	38
5.5	Action to be taken when acting for a third party	39
5.6	Dealing with directors	40
5.7	Position where s 35A does not apply	41
5.8	Ratification	41
5.9	Changing the objects clause	42

6 The Articles of Association — 43

6.1	The form of the articles of association	43
6.2	Modifications to Table A	43
6.3	Use of information technology by companies	45
6.4	The articles as a contract	47
6.5	Relationship between the board and the general meeting	48
6.6	Alteration of the articles	48

7 Share Capital and Dividends — 51

    7.1   Types of share capital — 51

    7.2   Authority to issue shares — 52

    7.3   Pre-emption provisions — 53

    7.4   Issue of shares at a premium or a discount — 54

    7.5   Financial assistance — 55

    7.6   Class rights — 58

    7.7   Redemption of shares — 59

    7.8   Purchase of a company's own shares — 62

    7.9   Alteration of share capital — 64

    7.10   Dividends — 64

8 Directors — 69

    8.1   Who can become a director — 69

    8.2   Types of directors — 69

    8.3   Appointment of directors — 70

    8.4   Termination of director's office — 71

    8.5   Directors' fiduciary duties — 73

    8.6   Duties of care and skill — 75

    8.7   Deals with directors — 77

    8.8   Disclosure — 79

    8.9   Single member companies — 79

    8.10   Disqualification of directors — 80

9 Meetings — 83

    9.1   Types of meetings — 83

    9.2   Convening general meetings — 83

9.3	Notices of general meeting	84
9.4	Types of resolutions	86
9.5	Representation at meetings	92
9.6	Proceedings at general meetings	92
9.7	Amendments to resolutions	95
9.8	Board meetings	95

10 The Elective Regime — 97

10.1	Introduction	97
10.2	The elective resolution	97
10.3	Requirements that can be dispensed with	98

11 Execution of Documents by a Company — 103

11.1	Introduction	103
11.2	Documents under hand	103
11.3	Documents under seal	104

12 Minority Shareholder Rights — 107

12.1	The rule in *Foss v Harbottle*	107
12.2	Section 459	108
12.3	Just and equitable winding-up	111

13 Charges and Debentures — 113

13.1	The power to borrow	113
13.2	Types of debentures	113
13.3	Circumstances in which a floating charge will crystallise	115
13.4	Priority of charges	115
13.5	Section A: registration of company charges	116

	13.6	Section B: reform	119
	13.7	Receivers	119

14 Company Law Reform — 121

	14.1	Introduction	121
	14.2	Private company law reform: proposals	121

15 Forms — 127

16 Useful Addresses — 139

17 Time Periods and Penalties — 141

18 Further Reading — 145

	18.1	Looseleaf works	145
	18.2	Books and official reports	145
	18.3	Journals	145

1 Sources and Definitions

1.1 Source material

The Companies Act 1985 contains the major consolidation of the law relating to both private and public companies, and its provisions incorporate many of those contained in the Companies Acts 1948, 1967, 1980 and 1981. The Act has been amended by the Companies Act 1989, but, even 11 years later, a number of its provisions still have not been (and will probably never be) brought into force. Further statutory provisions include the Business Names Act 1985, Insolvency Act 1986, Financial Services Act 1986, Company Directors Disqualification Act 1986 and Pt V of the Criminal Justice Act 1993, which contains the provisions relating to the prohibition of insider dealing. Underpinning these statutes is a morass of statutory instruments, including the Companies (Tables A to F) Regulations 1985 (SI 1985/805, as amended by SI 1985/1052); the Financial Services Act 1986 (Commencement) (No 13) Order 1995 (SI 1995/1538); the Companies and Business Name Regulations 1981 (SI 1981/1685, as amended by SI 1982/1653, SI 1992/1196 and SI 1995/3022); the Companies (Inspection and Copying of Registers, Indices and Documents) Regulations 1991 (SI 1991/1998); the Companies (Single Member Private Limited Companies) Regulations 1992 (SI 1992/1699); the Foreign Companies (Execution of Documents) Regulations 1994 (SI 1994/950 as amended by SI 1995/1729); and the Companies Act 1985 (Audit Exemption) (Amendment) Regulations 2000 (SI 2000/1430). References to a section number throughout this work are references to the Companies Act 1985, unless specific provision is made to the contrary.

1.2 Definitions

The Act	The Companies Act 1985 as amended by the Companies Act 1989.
Allotment of shares	The unconditional right for a person to be included in a company's register of members in respect of shares (s 738).
Alternate director	A person appointed by a director to act in his place and who is entitled to exercise the powers of a director to the extent permitted by the articles of association.
Annual general meeting or AGM	The general meeting, convened on at least 21 days' notice, which every company is required to hold within 18 months of incorporation and in every subsequent 15 month period (s 366), unless an elective resolution has been passed dispensing with such a requirement (s 366A) (see 'short notice'). The business conducted at an AGM will normally include approval of accounts, declaration of a dividend and appointment of directors and auditors.
Annual return	The form which is required to be submitted to the Registrar of Companies within 28 days of the first anniversary of the company's incorporation or the date on which the last return was made up, containing details of, amongst other things, share capital, shareholders and directors (ss 363–65).
Articles of Association	The regulations of a company which establish the rights and obligations of shareholders, the division of power between the general meeting and the board of directors and specify the administrative and procedural manner in which the company can conduct business (see 'Table A').

Authorised or nominal share capital	The share capital which is authorised by the memorandum of association, whether or not allotted or issued (see 'issued share capital').
Board of directors	The directors of a company acting collectively who will, invariably, be given the power in the articles of association to manage the business of the company.
Bonus or capitalisation issue	An issue of shares to existing shareholders *pro rata* to their holdings and paid up out of the reserves of the company, normally from an otherwise undistributable reserve, such as the share premium account.
Class rights	Rights that attach to a particular class of shares or are given to shareholders in their capacity as shareholders and which cannot be varied unless approval of the relevant class is obtained in accordance with the requirements of s 125 and, if appropriate, the memorandum and articles of association.
Call on shares	Demand by the company for a shareholder to pay the whole or part of the amount outstanding on any shares held by him (see 'partly paid shares').
Company secretary	A person who is generally responsible for ensuring that the administrative provisions of the articles of association and the Act are complied with, such as minuting board meetings and ensuring that the appropriate forms are registered with the Registrar of Companies.
Corporate representative	A representative who has been duly appointed by a company (whether or not incorporated under the Act) to attend and vote at a general meeting and who is treated as if he were an individual shareholder (s 375).

Debenture	Acknowledgment of a company's debt. The debt may be either unsecured or secured by a fixed or floating charge over its assets.
Director	A person appointed alone or together with others to manage the business of a company in accordance with the articles of association.
Dividend	Income distribution made out of 'profits available for the purpose' (as defined in s 263) and paid to shareholders in proportion to the number of, and in accordance with the rights attaching to, shares held by them.
DTI	The Department of Trade and Industry.
Elective regime	Those provisions introduced by the Companies Act 1989 which permit companies to dispense with certain administrative provisions of the Act by passing an appropriate elective resolution. This Act contemplates that legislation might be introduced in the future in order to allow companies to simplify compliance with, or avoid entirely, certain provisions of the Act.
Elective resolution	A resolution passed at a general meeting of shareholders held on at least 21 days' notice and agreed to at the meeting, in person or by proxy, by all shareholders entitled to attend and vote at the meeting, in order to dispense with certain administrative provisions of the Act (s 379A) (see 'written resolution').
Extraordinary general meeting	Any general meeting of shareholders other than the annual general meeting.
Extraordinary resolution	A resolution passed at a general meeting held on at least 14 days' notice and agreed to by not less than 75% of those shareholders present in person or by proxy at the meeting (s 378(1)) and required by the Insolvency Act 1986 to be used in circumstances relating to the

	winding-up of a company and used at meetings of a class of shareholders to vary class rights (see 'short notice', 'written resolution').
Fixed charge	A charge over specified assets as security for obligations owed to a third party which requires the consent of the third party before the company is able to dispose of the charged assets.
Floating charge	A charge over the general undertaking of a company's property as security for obligations owed to a third party which allows the company to freely deal with the assets which are the subject of the charge until an event of crystallisation occurs, usually, amongst other things, the appointment of a receiver or liquidator, when the charge becomes a fixed equitable charge.
General meeting	A meeting of shareholders which has the powers specified in the articles of association.
Issued share capital	The share capital of a company which has been issued to its shareholders (see 'authorised share capital', 'partly paid shares').
Limited liability company	A company in which a shareholder's liability to contribute to its assets in the event of the company having insufficient resources to discharge its debts is limited to any unpaid amount on his shares (see 'partly paid shares', 'unlimited company').
Liquidator	The person appointed to deal with the assets and liabilities of the company once the resolution to wind up has been passed or a compulsory winding-up order has been made (see 'winding-up').
Member or shareholder	The holder of shares in a company.

Memorandum of association	Constitutional document which sets out the company's name, whether the shareholders have limited liability, the country in which its registered office is to be located, the objects clause and its authorised share capital.
Objects clause	The clause in the memorandum of association which sets out the objects of the company and the powers which can be used for the attainment of such objects (see '*ultra vires*').
Officer	Includes the following persons: director, manager or secretary of a company (s 744).
Ordinary resolution	A resolution passed at a general meeting held on at least 14 days' notice and agreed to by a majority of those shareholders present in person or by proxy at the meeting. An ordinary resolution is used whenever the Act or the articles of association do not require the passing of an elective, extraordinary or special resolution (see 'short notice', 'written resolution').
Ordinary shares	Shares which have a residual right to receive dividends and the surplus on a winding-up after the payment of dividends or surplus to holders of preference shares.
Ostensible or apparent authority	The authority that an agent, such as a director, has to bind the company (in circumstances where he does not have actual authority to do so) by virtue of the agent being held out by the company as having the powers associated with the position held by him.
Partly paid shares	Shares in respect of which there is a liability to pay a sum of money which becomes due once demanded by the company (see 'call on shares').

Preference shares	Shares which are entitled to receive dividends and/or a specified amount on a winding-up in priority to holders of ordinary shares. Such shares do not normally carry a right to vote unless any specified dividend is in arrears.
Proxy	The authority given by a shareholder to another person (not necessarily another shareholder) to attend and vote in his place at a general meeting. A proxy has the same right to speak at the meeting as the shareholder who appointed him (s 372).
Ratification	The process whereby a voidable act of the company is validated by a resolution of shareholders or the board.
Shadow director	A person in accordance with whose directions or instructions the directors of a company are accustomed to act other than a person giving advice in a professional capacity (s 741, as clarified in *Secretary of State for Trade and Industry v Deverell and Another* [2000] 2 All ER 365; see discussion below, 8.2). Shadow directors are treated for certain provisions of the Act and the Insolvency Act 1986 as directors.
Share premium account	Where a company issues shares at a premium over their par value, the amount of any premium is, within the company's books of accounts, placed within the share premium account, which, for most purposes, is treated as if it were share capital (s 130 and see below, 7.4).
Short notice	The ability for ordinary, special and extraordinary resolutions (but not elective resolutions) to be passed at a general meeting notwithstanding that the usual notice period required by the Act has not been complied with. In order for a general meeting to be

	held on short notice, the consent of shareholders holding at least 95% in nominal value (or 90% if an appropriate elective resolution has been passed) of voting shares is required, save that, in the case of an annual general meeting, all the shareholders entitled to vote thereat must consent (ss 369, 378).
Special resolution	A resolution passed at a general meeting convened on at least 21 days' notice and agreed to by not less than 75% of those shareholders present in person or by proxy at the meeting (s 378(2)). A special resolution is required to sanction certain matters required by the Act (see 'short notice', 'written resolution' and below, 9.4.2).
Stamp duty	The tax payable, in absence of an appropriate exemption, on transfers of shares at the rate of 0.5% of the consideration monies.
Stock transfer form	The form recognised by the Stock Transfer Act 1963 for the purpose of transferring legal title to shares.
Subscription of shares	The issue of shares by the company to a person.
Table A	Those articles of association contained in Table A of the Companies (Tables A to F) Regulations 1985 (SI 1985/805, as amended by SI 1985/1052) which will be deemed to be a company's articles of association if no articles are registered, or, if registered, insofar as such articles do not exclude or modify Table A (s 8).
Ultra vires	The doctrine which provides that acts by a company outside its permitted objects contained in its objects clause will be void and unenforceable. The doctrine has been significantly restricted by the amendments to the Act introduced by the Companies Act 1989.

Unlimited company	A company in which shareholders have an unlimited liability to contribute to its assets in order to enable the company to discharge its debts.
Winding-up or liquidation	The procedure whereby the assets of a company are gathered in and realised, the liabilities met and the surplus, if any, distributed to shareholders.
Written resolution	A resolution signed by all the shareholders of a company entitled to vote at a general meeting for the purpose of effecting an ordinary, special or extraordinary resolution and, insofar as the procedure set out in ss 381A–381C is followed, an elective resolution.

2 Introduction

2.1 What is a private company?

The scope of this work is restricted to private companies and does not cover public companies or the special rules applicable to private companies that are subsidiaries of public companies. A private company is defined in the Act as a company other than a public company (s 1(3)). A public company is a limited company with a share capital which is identified as such in its memorandum of association and in respect of which the provisions of the Act have been complied with. A public company has to have a minimum issued share capital before it can commence trading and comply with certain additional formalities set out in the Act.

The main distinction between private and public companies is the restriction upon the marketing of private company shares:

- Section 81 (which has generally been repealed but remains in force for this purpose; see SI 1995/1538) provides that it is a criminal offence for a private limited company to:
  - offer its shares or debentures to the public;
  - allot or agree to allot shares or debentures with a view to all or any of those shares or debentures being offered to the public, that is, securities are allotted to an intermediary who on-sells to the public. There is a presumption that shares or debentures are being so offered if the securities were actually sold to the public within six months of the allotment or if at the time of the offer the company had not received the whole consideration for the shares or debentures (s 58).
- No assistance is given as to what constitutes an offer to the public. The Act merely provides that an offer to the public includes an offer to any section of the public (s 59).

- The Act provides that an offer will not constitute an offer to the public, and private limited companies will, accordingly, be able to make an offer of their shares, if the offer is:
  - not calculated to result, directly or indirectly, in the shares or debentures becoming available for subscription or purchase by persons other than those receiving the offer or invitation; or
  - otherwise purely of a domestic concern of the persons receiving and making it.
- There is a presumption that an offer is in the nature of a domestic concern if it is made to:
  - an existing shareholder or debenture holder;
  - an existing employee or the securities are to be held under an employees' share scheme;
  - a close family relation of any shareholder or employee as specified in s 60(5).
- The Public Offers of Securities Regulations (SI 1995/1537) came into force on 19 June 1995. These provide for persons offering certain securities to the public to prepare a prospectus complying with the Regulations. Although these Regulations are not of direct relevance to private companies, given their inability to offer shares to the public, they provide a number of exemptions as to what will not constitute a public offer. In particular, an offer is not considered to be made to the public if the securities are offered to less than 50 persons, nor if the securities are restricted to persons whom the offeror reasonably believes to be sufficiently knowledgeable to understand the risks involved in accepting the offer. In addition, the Regulations make it clear that an offer to those persons falling within the exemptions does not constitute an offer to the public. Although the definition of 'public offer' is only applicable for the purposes of the Regulations, it is hard to believe that a court would not take into account these provisions in interpreting what constitutes an offer to the public for the purpose of s 81.

In all other respects, a private company is able to carry out the same activities as a public company. In general, the formalities contained in the Act are less onerous for private companies than for public companies. For example, only private companies are able to avail themselves of the provisions contained in the Companies Act 1989 which enable them to reduce the administrative burden of complying with the Act (see below, Chapter 10). In addition, private companies (unlike public companies) do not require a minimum share capital, are not subject to the same restrictions on the payment of dividends and can, in specified circumstances, redeem their shares out of capital (see below, 7.8) and give financial assistance in connection with the purchase of their own shares (see below, 7.5). A private company may re-register as a public company, provided that the requirements set out in s 43 are complied with.

2.2 Types of private companies

A private company may be constituted so that the liability of its members may be either limited or unlimited. Members of a limited company are only liable to contribute to the assets of a company to the extent that any amount remains to be paid up on their shares. Usually, shares are issued fully paid, so that members will not have any further liability to contribute to the assets of the company. It should be stressed that a limited company will remain fully liable for its own debts; it is only the liability of members that is limited.

In contrast, members of an unlimited company, together with those who were members in the 12 months immediately prior to its winding-up in respect of debts incurred whilst they were members, will retain unlimited liability for the debts of a company (s 74 of the Insolvency Act 1986). Unlimited companies are normally established for the following reasons:

- where members wish to be able to withdraw capital from the company without the consent of the court (such consent being required for limited companies under s 135);
- where members wish to retain a degree of financial secrecy. An unlimited company does not have to file accounts with the Registrar of Companies provided that it is neither the parent nor the subsidiary of a limited company and the other requirements of s 254 are complied with;
- where it is not considered important to have limited liability, such as where a public company incorporates a subsidiary and believes it to be commercially appropriate for it to be seen as standing behind its subsidiary.

Liability of members in a private company may be limited either by shares or by guarantee. A company limited by guarantee does not have a share capital and its members are required to pay the company on a winding-up the amount that is necessary to discharge the company's debts, up to the maximum specified in the guarantee (s 74 of the Insolvency Act 1986). The obligation to pay under the guarantee applies to both existing members and those who were members within the 12 months immediately prior to the winding-up specified in the memorandum (Table C, para 5 of SI 1985/805, as amended (see above, 1.1)). Companies limited by guarantee are used in circumstances where it is not necessary for a company to have working capital for the purpose of trading and are frequently used by clubs, societies and schools and for charitable purposes.

2.3 The consequences of incorporation

The main advantage associated with using a private limited company as the vehicle for the conduct of business is the limited liability of its members in the event of the company being unable to pay its debts. However, this advantage should not be overstated, since, prior to the company establishing a reputable trading record, banks will want its principal shareholders to personally guarantee money lent by them to the company. In addition, incorporation (for both limited and unlimited companies) has the following advantages:

- a company is able to create a floating charge over its assets (see below, Chapter 13). This form of security is not available to individuals or partnerships and greatly facilitates a company raising finance;
- a company is a separate legal entity from its members and, therefore, it can sue and be sued, hold property and carry out most activities, subject to any limitations contained in its memorandum and articles of association, which a natural person could do;
- a company will remain in existence until it is wound up or dissolved and is unaffected by the death of or change in its members.

Against the advantages of incorporation it is necessary to balance the greater degree of formality with which private companies are required to comply. Companies have to comply with the provisions of the Act, which, at times, can be onerous – for example, the preparation and filing of audited accounts. Furthermore, compliance may require considerable management time and necessitate the appointment of outside advisers. In addition, a company must make certain information available to the public about its directors, shareholders and financial position (see below, Chapter 4).

2.4 Protection of creditors

Although a company is able to be incorporated with limited liability, company law recognises that dealing with such a company may involve a higher degree of commercial risk than dealing with an individual or partnership. Accordingly, the Act contains a number of provisions to ensure that creditors appreciate the nature of the entity with which they are dealing, enable them to assess the credit risk which they are taking and ensure that the company's funds are available for the payment of its debts. Therefore:

- All private limited companies must have 'limited' as the last word in their name (or the Welsh equivalent) (s 25) and each company's full name must be placed in a conspicuous position outside its registered office and on its notepaper and other official publications (ss 348, 349).

  The only limited exception is that non-profit making private companies engaged in work for charity or the public good can apply to the Secretary of State not to have the word 'limited' in their name (s 30).

- If any person signs or authorises to be signed any cheque, bill of exchange, promissory note, endorsement or other order for money or goods which does not contain the full name of the company, then he is guilty of a criminal offence and is personally liable for the debt incurred by the company (s 349(4)). This section has, traditionally, been strictly interpreted by the courts; so, for example, a cheque drawn by a director of L&R Agencies Ltd which omitted the '&' was held to result in personal liability. However, in *Jenice v Dan* [1993] BCLC 1349, the court held that it was prepared to be less strict if the error does not mislead a person into believing that he is dealing with a different company.

- A limited company is required to file annual accounts with the Registrar of Companies (see below, Chapter 4), although these often tend to be rather out of date and of little assistance to potential creditors. A private company has 10 months to file its accounts from its year end, but, even so, many companies fail to meet the deadline.

- Save in very restricted circumstances, a limited company is unable, without being wound up, to return capital to its members without the consent of the court. The court, in deciding whether or not to consent to the reduction, will have regard to the interests of creditors.

Salomon v Salomon & Co Ltd [1897] AC 22 firmly established the principle that a company is a separate legal entity from its incorporators. There are, however, a number of exceptions to this rule where the court will permit the veil of incorporation to be lifted to facilitate the 'prevention of injustice' and the members will be held to be personally responsible for the debts of the company. The principal circumstances in which the veil of incorporation will be lifted are discussed below, 2.5–2.6.

2.5 Statute

There are a number of cases where Parliament has determined that it is appropriate for shareholders or directors to be held liable to contribute to the assets of a company notwithstanding the doctrine of limited liability. However, the courts will only interpret legislation as lifting the veil where it contains an unequivocal statement of Parliament's intention to do so. The following are examples of legislation that lift the veil:

- A number of provisions in the Insolvency Act 1986 permit the court to hold the directors or shadow directors of a company responsible for its debts; for example:
  o where the directors are guilty of fraudulent or wrongful trading contrary to s 213 or s 214 respectively. Fraudulent trading occurs where a person carries on the business of a company with intent to defraud creditors. Similarly, a director or shadow director of an insolvent company will be liable for wrongful trading if he knew or ought to have concluded that there was no reasonable prospect that the company could avoid going into insolvent liquidation and thereafter failed to take every step to minimise the potential loss to the company's creditors;
  o under s 217 any director or shadow director of an insolvent company who, during the following five years, is involved in the formation or management of a company or business with the same or similar name will be personally jointly liable with the company for its debts. This was introduced to prevent the unscrupulous manager from putting a company into insolvent liquidation and then establishing another company which would continue to trade under the name of the insolvent company.
- Under s 15 of the Company Directors Disqualification Act 1986, if a director, in contravention of a disqualification order, is concerned in the management of a company, then he, and any other person concerned with the management who is willing to act on his instructions despite knowing that he is disqualified, is jointly and severally liable with the company for its debts.

2.6 Case law

There have been several instances where, under case law, the corporate veil has been lifted:

- Where the corporate form is used in order to defeat the purpose of a statute. For example, *Re Bugle Press Ltd* [1961] Ch 270 concerned the interpretation of (what is now) s 429, which enables a shareholder who, in specified circumstances, acquires 90% of a company's share capital compulsorily to acquire the minority's shares. In that case, two shareholders wished to buy out a third, but neither, on their own, had a sufficient number of shares to implement s 429. Accordingly, the two shareholders established a company to which they transferred their shares and the company attempted to utilise 429. The court held that the company was a mere sham and would not permit it to take advantage of the compulsory acquisition procedure.

- Where the company is formed for the purpose of avoiding a legal obligation that would otherwise attach to the incorporator. In *Jones v Lipman* [1962] 1 All ER 442, the defendant contracted to sell certain property and then decided to retain it. In order to avoid an order for specific performance, the property was transferred to a company controlled by the defendant. The court held that an order for specific performance would be made against the company, since it was the creature of the defendant. See, also, *Gilford Motor Co Ltd v Horne* [1933] Ch 935.

- Where a relationship of agency can be implied between the company and its incorporators so that they will be responsible as principals for the debts of the company. An agency relationship will not be implied purely from the fact that a company is controlled by a particular shareholder; it is necessary to demonstrate a loss of identity between the company and its incorporators (see *Smith, Stone and Knight v Birmingham Corp* [1939] 4 All ER 116). This was demonstrated by *Re FG (Films) Ltd* [1953] 1 WLR 483, where a subsidiary was treated as the agent of its parent because the court considered the subsidiary to be so undercapitalised as to be incapable of independent action. It should be noted that the implication of any agency relationship is not a true example of lifting the veil, since the court is expressly recognising the existence of two companies.

- Despite Lord Denning's *dicta* in *DHN Food Distributors Ltd v Tower Hamlets LBC* [1976] 1 WLR 852 that there was evidence of the courts being prepared to ignore separate legal entities of companies within a group, it is clear that no special rules apply to group companies. The House of Lords in *Woolfson v Strathclyde Regional Council* 1978 SC (HL) 90 did not follow *DHN* and confirmed the traditional position that the veil would only be raised where there was a 'façade concealing the true facts'. This view was confirmed in England by the Court of Appeal in *Adams v Cape Industries plc* [1990] Ch 433 and, indeed, the court emphasised that group companies were entitled to be organised in such a way that legal liabilities fell on one company rather than another. Unfortunately, the court did not give a view on when a company would be considered to be a façade, although it did consider that the motive behind a company's incorporation might be a highly relevant factor. Such an intention is, however, not in itself crucial, since an intention present at the time that the façade is used will suffice.

3 Formation

3.1 Matters to be considered prior to forming a company

In order to form a company, certain information is required from the client. The purpose for requesting the information is included in the square brackets after the relevant information:

- The name of the company [memorandum and articles, Form 10] (see below, Chapter 15).
- Principal activities of the company [memorandum].
- The postal address of the registered office [first board meeting, Form 10] (see below, Chapter 15).
- Details of first directors: (a) full name (and any previous forenames or surnames); (b) usual residential address; (c) date of birth; (d) business occupation; (e) nationality; and (f) name of companies of which the individual is currently a director or has been a director in the last five years other than dormant or group companies [first board meeting, Form 10] (see below, Chapter 15).
- Details of first secretary: (a) full name (and any previous forenames or surnames); and (b) usual residential address [first board meeting, Form 10] (see below, Chapter 15).
- Details of the interests of the directors, their spouses (unless such spouses are also directors) and their children under 18 in shares or debentures of the company or any member of the group [register of directors' interests].
- The amount of authorised share capital [memorandum and articles]. In particular, (a) whether, in addition to ordinary shares, preference shares are to be issued; (b) nominal value; (c) currency; and (d) number of shares to be issued.
- The amount of issued share capital [first board minutes, Form 88(2)] (see below, Chapter 15).

- Details of subscribers and additional shareholders: (a) full name; (b) residential address; (c) the number of shares held by each [first board minutes, register of members].
- The name and address of the auditors and bankers [first board minutes].
- Details of who is able to sign cheques and specimen signatures [first board minutes, bank mandate].
- Instructions on amendments to be made on Table A [articles] (see below, 6.2).
- The date on which the accounting reference period is to end [first board minutes, Form 225] (see below, 3.6).
- Is the company to elect to dispense with any or all of certain Companies Act procedural requirements [first board minutes, first general meeting] (see below, Chapter 10)?

Particular consideration needs to be given to the following matters.

3.1.1 Directors

A private company must have at least one director (s 282). Any person (including a company) can act as a director of a company, provided that he is not the subject of a disqualification order made by the court pursuant to the Company Directors Disqualification Act 1986. There is no minimum or maximum age for the appointment of a director, although if a minor is appointed as a director, whilst he would be able to contract on behalf of the company, the company or any third party would not be able to enforce contracts against him personally.

3.1.2 Secretary

Every company must have a secretary. Any person can become a secretary, save that the secretary cannot be: (a) a person who is also the sole director (s 283(2)); (b) a corporation the sole director of which is the sole director of the company (s 283(4)); or (c) the company's auditor (s 27(1) of the Companies Act 1989).

3.1.3 Auditors

Every company is required to appoint auditors, whose principal duty is to audit the company's accounts to ensure that they provide a true and fair view of the company's affairs and otherwise comply with the requirements of the Act. In order to be appointed as an auditor, a person must have the qualifications set out in ss 30–33 of the Companies Act 1989.

3.1.4 Name

The name of the company must, if it is limited by shares, end with the word 'Limited' or 'Ltd' (s 25). A company is permitted to register with any name unless:

- The name is the same as or, in the opinion of the Secretary of State, too like a name already appearing on the register of companies. If a company with such name is registered the Secretary of State has 12 months from the date of registration to direct that the company change its name (s 28(2)). When deciding whether a name is the 'same as' another name, punctuation, the company's status and words like 'company (or co)', 'and (or &) company (or co)' will be ignored for the purposes of comparison. A name may be considered as too like another if it is phonetically identical to that other name or there is only a slight difference in spelling. This restriction does not extend to cases of 'implied association' where any company could be believed to be associated (for example, as a subsidiary) with another company already on the register. In addition, the person objecting to a 'too like' name will have to provide evidence that the new name will cause confusion between the company with that name and the company with the existing name in the minds of the public. The power to direct a company to change its name has rarely been used by the Secretary of State.
- The use of the name would, in the opinion of the Secretary of State, constitute a criminal offence (for example, the use of the word 'bank' where the company was not authorised under the Banking Act 1989), be offensive, or (unless the consent of the Secretary of State is obtained) the name is such that it would suggest that the company is connected with the government or a local authority (s 26(2)).
- The name includes one or more of the words listed in the Companies and Business Name Regulations 1981 (SI 1981/1685, as amended (see above, 1.1)) unless the consent of the relevant government department specified therein has first been obtained. For instance, use of the words 'Royal', 'International' and 'English' all require consent before a company can be registered with those words included in its name.
- It should be noted that, even if a company is registered with a particular name, it does not prejudice any other person's proprietary right to use that name. Accordingly, a passing off action or an action

for infringement of a trademark may be brought against a company if it trades under its registered name. If a company wishes to trade under its registered name, it should carry out a trademark search and make enquiries as to whether any third party is using the proposed name in the same field of activity as that proposed by the company.

3.1.5 Registered office

Every company must have a registered office within the locality specified in its memorandum of association (that is, England and Wales, Wales or Scotland) (s 287, as substituted by s 136 of the Companies Act 1989). The address of the registered office must be stated on the company's notepaper and order forms. Documents can be served on a company by leaving them at, or sending them by post to, the registered office (s 725). Furthermore, the company is required to keep certain information required by the Act available for public inspection at its registered office (see below, 3.5). Changes to the registered office can only be effected by giving notice on Form 287 to the Registrar. It is important to note that the change only takes effect upon the notice being 'registered by the Registrar' and not merely when the form is submitted to the Registrar. This may cause difficulties in practice, since it is not possible, with any accuracy, to determine the point in time at which the form is registered. In addition, it should be noted that documents can still be effectively served at the old registered office for a period of 14 days after the change has been registered. Clients should be warned of this provision and ensure that proper forwarding facilities for mail are put in place for this period of time.

3.1.6 Authorised and issued share capital

It is necessary to determine the amount of the company's authorised and issued share capital. The authorised share capital is the amount of share capital stated in the memorandum of association which is available to be issued. A company's authorised share capital can be increased by the passing of an ordinary resolution (s 123). The issued share capital is the amount of share capital issued to members that may equal but must not exceed the authorised share capital, and its amount will depend on the level of capital which a company will need to trade and the extent to which debt finance can be obtained from third parties. It may be helpful when forming a company to have an authorised share capital that will exceed the amount intended to be issued, since this will avoid the need for the share capital to be increased at a later stage. It is also possible to reduce a company's authorised share capital (by the passing of an ordinary resolution) by way of a cancellation of shares, which, at the date of the passing of the resolution, have not been taken or agreed to be taken by any person, and subdivide its shares into shares of smaller amount than is fixed by the memorandum (s 121). A cancellation of shares under s 121 does not, for the purposes of the Act, constitute a reduction of share capital requiring court approval.

3.1.7 The first shareholders or subscribers

A private company need only have a single shareholder (s 24, as amended by the Companies (Single Member Private Limited Companies) Regulations 1992 (SI 1992/1699)).

3.2 Formation of a company

3.2.1 Tailor-made companies

It takes approximately five working days for a company to be incorporated by the Registrar of Companies, at a cost of £20 (to which needs to be added the professional time for preparation of the necessary documents). Alternatively, a company is able to be incorporated on a same day basis for a fee of £100. A company comes into existence on the issue of a certificate of incorporation, which requires the following documents to be registered with the Registrar (together with the appropriate registration fee):

- The memorandum and, unless Table A is being adopted without amendment (see below, 6.1), articles of association, which have to be signed by the shareholder(s) who are subscribing for shares in the company and duly witnessed.
- Form 10 – statement of first directors and secretary and intended situation of registered office. The details that must be included concerning the proposed directors are their names, usual residential address, date of birth, business occupation and nationality. In addition, directors are required to give particulars of all current directorships. Details of directorships of companies that have been dormant (within the meaning of s 249AA) throughout the five year period or companies within the same group are not required to be included. The directors and secretary are required to sign the form as an indication of their consent to be appointed and, in addition, the form must be signed by or on behalf of the subscribers.

- Form 12 – statutory declaration of compliance with requirements on application for registration of a company. This declaration is to be made by the solicitor acting for the company or by any of the directors or the secretary named in Form 10, certifying that all the requirements of the Act in connection with, and incidental to, the formation of the company have been complied with. The declaration must be sworn in front of a solicitor, Commissioner for Oaths, Notary Public or Justice of the Peace. Examples of both sets of forms, completed, are set out below, Chapter 15.

3.2.2 Ready made or off-the-shelf companies

Where a company is needed on short notice, it is possible to purchase a ready made company from a company formation agent. The agent will, for a fee of approximately £150, provide a company that has already been incorporated with the objects that have been requested. It will be necessary to adapt the company for the particular needs of the client by (so far as may be necessary) changing its name, amending the memorandum and/or articles of association, increasing the share capital, appointing directors and a secretary and changing the registered office. The agents will provide a certificate of incorporation, confirmation that the company has not previously traded and stock transfer form(s) signed in blank by the subscriber(s), which need to be completed with the details of the transferee. In addition, first board minutes may be provided, recording the resignation of the first directors and secretary and appointing those specified by the client and resolving to change the registered office. The agent will normally require that the appropriate form (Form 288) is signed by the new directors and secretary, confirming their appointment and acknowledging the retirement of the old directors and secretary. These should be returned to the agent for filing at Companies House before they will permit the client to have control of the company. The introduction of company incorporations on a 'same day' basis has reduced the need for shelf companies. However, off-the-shelf companies may be more convenient where ready access to Companies House is not available.

3.3 Company notepaper

The company must put its full name on all business correspondence, notices, other official publications and on all cheques, bills of exchange, promissory notes, etc (s 349). In addition, it must include on its business letters and order forms its place of registration and the address of its registered office and its registration number. Where a company trades under a name other than its registered name, then it must, in addition to the requirements specified above, comply with the Business Names Act 1985. This Act, which overlaps with the requirement of the Companies Act 1985, requires that its corporate name and address for service must be stated on all business letters, invoices, receipts and written demands for the payment of debts (s 4). The restrictions contained in the Companies and Business Names Regulations 1981 (SI 1981/1685, as amended) (see above, 3.1.4) apply equally to trading names as to company names and the consent of the Secretary of State must be obtained if the trading name would give the impression that the company is connected with the government or any local authority. Failure to comply with the requirements of this Act is a criminal offence.

3.4 Publicity of name

The name of the company must be painted or affixed outside every office or place in which its business is carried on, in a conspicuous position and in letters easily legible (s 348). In addition, the name under which the company is trading is required to be prominently displayed at any business premises to which customers or suppliers are given access (s 4 of the Business Names Act 1985).

3.5 Company books

The secretary is responsible for ensuring that the information required by the Act is properly recorded and retained, although, of course, this responsibility may be delegated to company agents. The information that is required to be kept by the company is as follows:

- A register of members in which is to be recorded the names and addresses of shareholders, the dates upon which they became and ceased to be members and the number of shares held (s 352). If there are more than 50 members, and the entries are not included alphabetically, an index of members is required to be drawn up (s 354). Any alteration in the register of members should take place forthwith upon a person becoming or ceasing to be a member (no specific time limit is specified in the Act) and any amendment to the index must be made within 14 days of that date. Furthermore, if the number of shareholders on the register falls to one, then, in addition to the name and address of the single shareholder, the register has to include a statement that the company has only one member and the date on which that occurred. Conversely, if a company's membership increases beyond one, then there has to be included a statement that the company has ceased to have one member and the date on which that occurred (s 352A). This is intended to highlight to third parties that special rules will be applicable to such companies (see below, 8.9).

- A register of directors and secretaries (s 288), which is required to include the information on such officers specified in s 289 and is, broadly, the information required to be included in Form 10 (see above, 3.2.1). Details of any changes must be recorded within 14 days of their occurrence.
- A register of interests of directors and their families in the shares and debentures of the company or any company within the group (s 325), which records the information that a director is required to disclose pursuant to s 324 (see below, 8.8). A director must notify the company within five days of the appropriate event and such information is required to be included within three days of the notification (Sched 13, paras 14 and 22).
- A register of charges, which records all fixed and floating charges over the company's property (s 407) (see below, 13.5).
- Minutes of all proceedings of general meetings, directors' meetings and managers' meetings (s 382).

In general, all of the above information is required to be kept at the registered office, although the register of members and interests of directors can be kept elsewhere within the country of incorporation if the work done in respect of updating these registers takes place other than at the registered office. The registers and the minutes of a company's general meetings are to be available for inspection by shareholders for not less than two hours between 9 am and 5 pm on each business day and the person inspecting the registers must be allowed to take notes or transcribe the information. However, the company is not obliged to provide any other facilities to facilitate inspection, such as a dictating machine or photocopier. The fees payable for inspection of the relevant information are set out in the Companies (Inspection and Copying of Registers, Indices and Documents) Regulations 1991 (SI 1991/1998). The registers are not required to be in any prescribed form, provided that they contain the information required by the Act. Combined registers can be purchased from law stationers. Although not required by the Act, a company may wish to keep a register of debenture holders and a register of applications, allotments and transfers.

3.6 Matters to be dealt with at first board meeting

Immediately after the company is incorporated, it will be necessary for a board meeting to be convened, at which the following matters need to be addressed:

* the appointment of a chairman of the company, auditors and bankers and any additional directors;
* the directors may wish to notify the company of contracts that they are to be treated as generally interested in for the purpose of s 317 (see below, 8.5) and to provide the company with information about their and their families' shareholdings in the company to be included in the register required by s 325;
* where the register of members, register of directors' interests and copies of directors' service agreements required to be available for inspection pursuant to s 318 are to be kept. These will usually be kept at the registered office, but may be kept at any office where the compilation of the register of members is carried out;
* the adoption of a company seal (if required) (see below, Chapter 11);
* the date that is to be the financial year end of the company. Notification is required to be given to the Registrar on Form 225. In absence of such notice, the financial year end is deemed to be the last day of the month in which the anniversary of incorporation falls. The first accounting reference period must be between six and 18 months long (s 224);
* allot and issue the subscriber shares and (if necessary) approve the transfer of such shares. (If necessary,) convene a general meeting of shareholders for the purposes set out below. (After the general meeting has been held,) issue additional shares.

The above list will need to be adapted if a ready made company is purchased, since a number of these matters may already have been carried out by the company formation agents before the company is taken over.

3.7 First general meeting of the company

At the first meeting of shareholders, the following resolutions may be passed, depending on whether or not a ready made company has been purchased:

- special resolutions to:
  - change the name of the company
  - alter the memorandum and/or articles; and
  - disapply s 89 in relation to issues of shares (see below, Chapter 7);
- ordinary resolutions to:
  - increase the authorised share capital; and
  - authorise the directors to issue shares pursuant to s 80 (see below, Chapter 7);
- elective resolutions to dispense with certain requirements of the Companies Act (see below, Chapter 10).

4 The Companies Register

4.1 Company searches

Information that companies are required to file in accordance with the Act (see below, 4.3 and Chapter 15) is able to be inspected, in respect of companies registered in England and Wales, at Companies House in London and Cardiff and, in respect of companies registered in Scotland, at Companies House in Edinburgh. In addition, Companies House has satellite offices in Manchester, Birmingham, Leeds and Glasgow for personal searches to be conducted. The addresses and the telephone numbers of the relevant offices, together with the appropriate opening times, are set out below, Chapter 16. In order to make a search at Companies House, it is necessary to know the full name and registered number of the company in respect of which the search is to be carried out. This information can be obtained from the company's certificate of incorporation or change of name or, alternatively, from the company's notepaper, which is required by the Act to include the relevant information. If the company's name is known but not its registered number, then this information can be obtained from the public index of all companies kept at Companies House. A company search may be carried out in any of the following manners.

4.1.1 Companies House Direct

Companies House Direct is the computerised search system of Companies House, providing online access to information relating to the 1.2 million companies on the Register. It is accessible either by subscription, or in person at Companies House in Cardiff, Edinburgh or London, or at any of the satellite offices (addresses and contact details are given below, Chapter 16).

The procedure for conducting a personal search is as follows:
- obtain from the counter staff at Companies House a plastic 'search card' and make payment of the fee to cover searches to be carried out. Any amount can be paid on the card, with any unused amount being available for future use;
- following the instructions on-screen, enter the name and registered number of the company against which the search is to be made, and, after receiving confirmation as to the identity of the company, request a search;
- the service offers a choice of delivery options for documents requested – they can be viewed on-screen (the most common choice), or delivered by post or fax;
- there is no charge for viewing basic company details, or for checking whether a company is insolvent or a director is disqualified;
- the cost of viewing or downloading the first document is £2.50; any other document viewed at the same time relating to the same company costs £1. The cost of viewing a document is displayed on-screen;
- a fee of £9 is payable to receive a document by post; £12 by fax (further documents requested at the same time for the same company are £2.50 by post, £8 by fax);
- the online service can also be used to order older documents on microfiche. These can either be collected in person at a cost of £5, or posted at a cost of £8. Microfiche readers are provided at all locations.

4.1.2 Other search methods

It is still possible (though decreasingly common) to request a search by telephone or fax for postal or fax delivery. The same charges apply as for postal and fax delivery online. Payment must be made beforehand, or alternatively credit cards (Mastercard, Visa) can be used or an account opened with Companies House from which the necessary fees can be deducted. A minimum deposit of £100 is required to open an account.

Requests for postal delivery received by 3 pm will be despatched the same day by first class post; requests for fax delivery received by 4 pm will be transmitted within one hour of receipt. Details of the relevant telephone and fax numbers are set out below, Chapter 16.

4.2 Who to ask at Companies House

Companies House in Cardiff and Edinburgh are divided into a number of different departments, such as new companies, change of name, mortgage registration and document examination. As a first step, any question should be directed to the Central Enquiry Unit (Cardiff direct telephone: 02920 380801; Edinburgh: 0131 535 5800).

4.3 Matters required to be registered

Within 15 days of the passing of any of the following resolutions, a printed copy, signed by an officer of the company, must be filed with the Registrar:

- special resolutions (s 380(4)(a));
- extraordinary resolutions (s 380(4)(b));
- an elective resolution or any resolution revoking such a resolution (s 380(4)(bb));
- resolutions increasing the authorised share capital of the company (s 123);
- resolutions or agreements which have been agreed to by all the shareholders but, if not so agreed, would not have been effective for their purpose unless a special or extraordinary resolution had been passed (s 380(4)(c)). For example, a written resolution signed by all the shareholders may be required to be registered;
- resolutions or agreements which have been agreed to by all the members of some class of shareholders but which, if not so agreed to, would not have been effective for their purpose unless passed by some particular majority or otherwise in some particular manner and all resolutions or agreements which bind all members of a class, though not agreed to by all members (s 380(4)(d)). For example, registration is required where the holders of three-quarters in nominal value of any class of shares consent in writing to a variation of their class rights pursuant to s 125 (see below, 7.6);
- resolutions to give, vary, revoke or renew an authority to the directors to allot shares for the purposes of s 80 (s 380(4)(f)) (see below, 7.2);
- resolutions conferring, varying, revoking or renewing authority for a company to purchase its own shares pursuant to s 166 (s 380(4)(h)) (see below, 7.8);
- a resolution for a voluntary winding-up (s 380(4)(j)).

A number of other resolutions that are required to be filed are set out in s 380.

Details of further matters to be filed at Companies House are set out below, Chapter 7.

4.4 Constructive notice

In the circumstances in which s 35A applies (see below, Chapter 5), a person will not be deemed to have constructive knowledge of the memorandum and articles of association or other documents filed at Companies House relating to a company's capacity to enter into a particular transaction (indeed, a person will not be treated as having knowledge of the contents of such documents, even if he has read them!). In situations where s 35A does not apply or is not relevant, a person will be treated as having constructive knowledge of a company's constitutional documents filed at Companies House and, possibly, other information on a company's file. The position will, in theory, change if and when ss 416 and 711A, which have been introduced by the Companies Act 1989, come into force. It should be noted, however, that these provisions were originally intended to become effective in 1991 and have been subsequently delayed whilst the DTI reviews the position (see below, 13.6). At present, there remains no specified date for the implementation of the relevant parts of the Companies Act 1989.

Section 711A(1) deals with all other matters on the Register, other than the Register of Charges, and provides: 'A person shall not be taken to have notice of any matter merely because of its being disclosed in any document kept by the Registrar of Companies (and thus available for inspection) or made available by the company for inspection.' However, this provision is rather importantly qualified by the following sub-section: 'This does not affect the question whether a person is affected by notice of any matter by reason of a failure to make such inquiries as ought reasonably to be made.' This qualification effectively negates s 711A, since it will never be possible to conclude with any certainty whether in any particular circumstance a company search need not be made. Presumably, this sub-section was intended to ensure that professionals such as banks and insurance companies were not treated in the same favourable manner as less commercially experienced third parties, but the effect has been to throw doubt on the precise ambit of s 711A so that, if the section ever comes into force, it will usually still be necessary to search the register.

4.5 Compliance

Generally, failure to comply with the registration requirements of the Act will result in all officers of the company who are in default and the company itself being guilty of a criminal offence and being liable for a fine (see below, Chapter 7). Recent years have seen many small companies in default of a number of the Act's provisions and the Registrar is enforcing the filing requirements more vigorously than he has done in the past. On average, 1,300 directors are convicted each year for such an offence. As an alternative to prosecution, the Registrar may, if appropriate returns are not made for long periods of time, assume that the company is no longer in business and strike it off the Register pursuant to s 652. This is, obviously, a serious step and can only be remedied by an application to the court on behalf of the company concerned.

5 The Memorandum of Association and the Doctrine of *Ultra Vires*

5.1 The contents of the memorandum

A memorandum of association must contain the following information (s 2):

- the full name of the company;
- whether the registered office is to be located in England and Wales, Wales or Scotland;
- the objects of the company;
- whether the liability of members is to be limited and, if it is a company limited by guarantee, the amount which each member is liable to contribute on a winding-up;
- the amount of authorised share capital and its division between different classes of shares;
- the class and number of shares which each subscriber is to take up.

In addition, the memorandum must be signed by the subscribers in the presence of a witness, who must also attest his signature.

5.2 The objects clause

The objects clause consists of a number of paragraphs that set out the objects for which a company was established, together with the powers necessary to achieve those objects. Objects clauses, traditionally, tend to be very long and cover almost all activities which a company could wish to carry out.

Historically, a distinction has been made between objects and powers in an objects clause. Objects are the primary objectives of the company, whereas powers are the means by which such objectives are achieved. Powers may only be used for the fulfilment of the objects and any other use, whilst not *ultra vires*, is an abuse by the directors of their powers (*Rolled Steel Products (Holdings) Ltd v British Steel Corp* [1986] Ch 246). Accordingly, it became important to construe the memorandum in order to discover whether the problem arose from a lack of capacity (that is, the act was outside the objects) or a lack of authority (that is, use of a power by the directors for an improper or unauthorised purpose). There are a number of points to note in relation to the interpretation of the objects clause:

- Even if a particular power is not expressed, a court will imply all the powers that are necessary or conducive to the attainment of a company's main objects (*AG v Great Eastern Rly Co* (1880) 5 App Cas 473).
- Whilst it is not legitimate to specify that a company has all the powers of a natural person, a company is able to include in its objects clause the right for the company to carry on any trade or business which, in the opinion of its board of directors, could be advantageously carried on in connection with or ancillary to its main business (*Bell Houses Ltd v City Wall Properties Ltd* [1966] 2 QB 656).
- Problems have arisen in the past from the courts interpreting all the paragraphs following the main objects as powers to be used for the fulfilment of the main objects. Accordingly, a paragraph is included at the end of the objects clause expressing that each clause is to be treated as an independent object (*Cotman v Brougham* [1918] AC 514). It should be noted that, whilst courts accept the legitimacy of such a clause, its effects will not necessarily be to change all the powers into objects. The rule is that all paragraphs will be treated as substantive objects unless:
  - the subject matter of the paragraph is by its nature incapable of constituting a substantive object. For example, *Re Introductions* [1970] Ch 199 held that a power to borrow money was (save in the case of a bank or money lending institution) incapable of being an object and had to be treated as a power;
  - the wording of the paragraph shows expressly or by implication that the paragraph was intended to be a power. For example, in *Rolled Steel Products (Holdings) Ltd v British Steel Corp* [1986] Ch 246, the court was construing a paragraph that gave the company the ability to give guarantees in favour of such persons 'as may seem expedient'. The court held that this constituted a power, since it could only mean 'as may seem expedient for the furtherance of the objects of the company'.

Section 3A permits a company to state that its object is to carry on business as a general commercial company, and this will permit the company to carry on any trade or business whatsoever. In such a case, the company is deemed to have power to do all such things as are incidental or conducive to the carrying on of trade or business by it. It is probably best to avoid using such a clause by itself, since it is necessary to make it clear beyond doubt that a company has power to do a particular act (in particular, the giving of guarantees and charitable or political donations) and not rely on a judicial interpretation as to whether an act was 'incidental or conducive to the carrying on of any trade or business by it'.

5.3 The doctrine of *ultra vires*

The doctrine of *ultra vires* provides that any act of a company outside its permitted objects is void and cannot be enforced by or against third parties. The Act attempts to abolish the doctrine of *ultra vires* in relation to third parties, although it expressly retains the doctrine with regard to shareholders, so that they are still able to bring an action against directors for *ultra vires* acts.

Section 35(1) provides: 'The validity of an act done by a company shall not be called into question on the ground of lack of capacity by reason of anything in the company's memorandum.' The following should be borne in mind when considering this section:

- A shareholder is able to obtain an injunction against the company in respect of acts proposed to be done outside the objects clause. However, no injunctive proceedings can be brought in respect of an act that is required to be done in fulfilment of a legal obligation arising from a previous act of the company. Accordingly, if, for example, a company enters into a contract to purchase land, being an act outside its objects clause, then a shareholder will not be able to obtain an injunction to prevent the company from completing the purchase.
- This section does not affect any liability that the directors may incur as a result of their authorising the company to perform an act outside the memorandum. However, an act outside a company's objects clause is able to be ratified by a special resolution of shareholders and if shareholders' approval is obtained in advance, no injunctive proceedings will be able to be brought, nor, depending on the terms of the resolution, will the shareholders have a claim against the directors.

- The benefits of this section do not apply where a director of a company or its holding company or a person connected with him is the person dealing with the company (see below, 5.6).

5.4 Dealings by a third party with officers of the company

Section 35A(1) provides:

> In favour of a person dealing with a company in good faith, the power of the board of directors to bind the company, or authorise others to do so, shall be deemed to be free of any limitation under the company's constitution.

A person is treated as dealing with a company if he is a party to any transaction or other act to which the company is a party, which includes being the recipient of a gift from the company.

Section 35A(2)(b) provides that a person shall not be regarded as acting in bad faith by reason only of his knowing that an act is beyond the powers of the directors under the company's constitution. Accordingly, the fact that a third party had actual knowledge of the contents of the memorandum or articles of association will not itself deprive him of protection if he honestly and reasonably failed to appreciate that they had the effect of precluding the company (or any director or other person acting on its behalf) from entering into the transaction. This is designed to afford protection to corporate third parties, for example, a bank where one branch has knowledge of a company's memorandum but the branch making the loan does not. Similarly, it will protect a third party who, although he has knowledge of the memorandum, fails to understand its implications. Therefore, in order for a person to lose the protection of s 35A, it will be necessary for the company to show that he has actual knowledge of the company's or directors' lack of capacity and that, armed with this knowledge, it can be proved that he acted otherwise than in good faith. For example, if the third party knew that the directors knew that they were acting outside their authority derived from the company's constitution, this may deprive him of the protection of s 35A.

Section 35A protects third parties from lack of authority derived from 'any limitation under the company's constitution', which includes limitations deriving from a resolution of the company in general meeting or from any agreement between the members or of any class of members (that is, written resolutions and those requiring to be filed pursuant to s 380(4)(c) and (d)) (see above, 4.3).

Accordingly, s 35A will be of no assistance in the following cases:
- where the act is illegal, for instance, where the directors authorise the company to give financial assistance in connection with the purchase by the company of its own shares contrary to s 151 (see below, 7.5);
- where the directors act in breach of their fiduciary duties and it is claimed that a third party has received the company's property in knowledge of the breach of duty and is a constructive trustee;
- where the limitation arose from a resolution of the board itself. So, for example, if the board passes a resolution prohibiting the finance director from entering into contracts for more than £1,000 and the finance director does so, then s 35A will not be relevant in determining whether the third party can enforce the contract because this is not a limitation under the company's constitution; the third party will be required to rely on the traditional ostensible authority rules (see below, 5.7).

5.5 Action to be taken when acting for a third party

As a result of a number of difficulties with the legislation, some of which are outlined in 5.4, above, it is still necessary if acting for a third party in dealing with a company to obtain and review:
- board minutes of the company authorising a relevant individual or class of individual to enter into the transaction. A minute signed by the chairman of the board meeting is evidence of the proceedings (s 382(2));
- a company search, in order to determine whether the directors have been properly appointed and ensure that no receiver, administrator or liquidator has been appointed which would restrict the directors' powers; s 35A may not provide adequate protection in such a case and a third party may have constructive knowledge of the contents of the register, notwithstanding s 711A(1), if and when it comes into force (see above, 4.4);
- the articles of association, in order to determine whether there are any special requirements for the execution of documents. Again, s 35A may not extend to procedural formalities.

5.6 Dealing with directors

The main exception to s 35A is where one or more of the parties to the transaction is a director of a company or its holding company or connected or associated therewith (as such terms are defined by s 346 and include, for example, close relatives and companies where the directors control at least 20% of the equity shares) and the board of directors, in connection with the transaction, exceeds any limitation on its powers under the company's constitution. In such a case, the director will not be entitled to rely upon s 35A. Section 322A provides that such transactions as between the company and the director or connected party are voidable at the instance of the company unless previously authorised or subsequently ratified.

Whether or not the transaction is avoided (unless it has been ratified; see below, 5.8), the party to the transaction and any director who authorised it is liable to account to the company and to indemnify the company against any loss suffered. The transaction ceases to be voidable if:

- restitution is no longer possible;
- the company is indemnified against any loss or damage arising from the transaction;
- a third party, without notice of the directors' lack of authority, acquires rights which would be prejudiced if the contract was avoided;
- the transaction is ratified by an ordinary or special resolution.

Where a person other than a director (that is, one of the connected or associated parties) is also a party to the contract, he has a defence if he can demonstrate that, at the time of the transaction, he did not know that the directors were exceeding their powers. Furthermore, where there are a number of parties to the transaction in question, some of which have the protection of s 35A and some of which do not, the court has a general discretion to affirm or set aside the transaction on such terms as appear to it just.

When acting for a director who is dealing with his company, it will be necessary, in addition to the steps outlined in 5.5, above, to review the memorandum and articles to ensure that the company has the appropriate authority to enter into the transaction. In addition, regard must also be had to those matters set out below, 8.7.

5.7 Position where s 35A does not apply

Where s 35A is not applicable (see above, 5.4), whether a company will be bound by the act of a director who did not have actual (expressed or implied) authority to do so will depend on the rules relating to ostensible authority. The well known case of *Freeman & Lockyer v Buckhurst Park Properties (Mangal) Ltd* [1964] 2 QB 480 laid down the requirements for ostensible authority to exist:

- That a representation that the agent had authority to enter on behalf of the company into a contract of the kind sought to be enforced was made to the other party. This representation is usually made by the board permitting a person to occupy a particular position within the company, for example, managing director.
- That such representation was made by a person or persons who had 'actual' authority to manage the business of the company either generally or in respect of those matters to which the contract relates.
- That he (the contractor) was induced by such representations to enter into the contract, that is, that he in fact relied upon it.
- That under its memorandum or articles of association the company was not deprived of the capacity either to enter into a contract of the kind sought to be enforced or to delegate authority to enter into a contract of that kind to the agent. This requirement will be substantially reduced if s 711A is introduced (see above, 4.4).

Provided that these requirements are fulfilled, a third party can enforce a contract against a company even though the relevant officer did not have actual authority to bind the company.

5.8 Ratification

The distinction between objects and powers (determined in accordance with the rules set out above, 5.2) remains relevant for the purpose of ratification. If the directors are acting outside the objects of the company, then their action can only be ratified by a special resolution (s 35(3)). Furthermore, if the directors wish to be relieved from personal liability in respect of the unauthorised transaction, this must be done by separate resolution, so that shareholders have the opportunity to affirm the act without, necessarily, releasing the directors from liability. If, however, the directors are acting within the objects but outside their powers, then, since it is not a matter relating to corporate capacity, the transaction concerned can be ratified by an ordinary resolution.

5.9 Changing the objects clause

A company may, by special resolution, alter its objects (s 4). However, a minority holding 15% of the company's share capital may, within 21 days of the passing of the resolution, object to any amendment to the objects clause. The court has power to set the amendment aside or confirm the amendment in whole or in part on such terms and conditions as it may think appropriate, including ordering the company to purchase the minorities' shares (s 4). It should be remembered that acts outside the objects clause may now be ratified by 75% of the shareholders present at the meeting and, whilst such a minority could prevent a change in the objects clause, they would be unable to stop the company ratifying an act which took place outside the memorandum. This may, however, give rise to a remedy under general law for protection of minority shareholders (see below, Chapter 12).

6 The Articles of Association

6.1 The form of the articles of association

The articles of association contain those regulations of a company that establish the rights and obligations of shareholders, the division of power between the general meeting and the board of directors and regulate the administrative and procedural manner in which the company can conduct business.

There are currently standard sets of articles contained in Companies (Tables A to F) Regulations 1985 (SI 1985/805, as amended (see above, 1.1)) which can be incorporated with or without modification. Table A is a form of articles for a company limited by shares and will become the articles of a limited company if no articles are registered; or, if articles are registered, Table A will apply to the extent that such articles do not modify or exclude Table A (s 8). Private companies limited by guarantee without a share capital and unlimited companies must have their articles in the form set out in Tables C or E respectively, or as near to that form as circumstances permit.

The Companies Act 1985 (Electronic Communications) Order 2000 (SI 2000/3373), which came into force on 22 December 2000 (made pursuant to s 8 of the Electronic Communications Act 2000, enacted in July 2000), amends the Act to enable companies to use electronic means to deliver company communications. The implications of these provisions on Table A are discussed below, 6.3.

6.2 Modifications to Table A

Many private companies adopt articles that incorporate a modified Table A. The usual amendments made to Table A are as follows:

- If particular rights are to be attached to shares, these will need to be set out in either the memorandum or the articles of association.
- The directors may be given power in the articles to allot and issue shares pursuant to s 80 (alternatively, this authority may be conferred by ordinary resolution at a general meeting) and it is usual to exclude the statutory pre-emption provisions contained in s 89 (see below, Chapter 7).
- Pre-emption provisions may be included so that, if a shareholder wishes to sell his shares (other than, usually, a sale to close relatives or related companies), he must first offer them to existing shareholders prior to a sale to a third party. The articles would specify the procedure for making the offer and the manner in which the price is to be calculated. It is usual for the price to be calculated by reference to a specified formula based at a relevant date or, alternatively, be determined by the auditors using the assumptions set out in the relevant article.
- Provision might be included to provide for certain categories of business at an AGM to constitute 'ordinary business', which obviates the need to give shareholders express notice of such matters (see below, 9.3.3).
- If it is intended that proxies can vote on a show of hands, reg 54 will have to be amended.
- Regulation 62 of Table A requires that a form of proxy is deposited at least 48 hours before the holding of a general meeting. In small companies, this provision may be considered unduly restrictive, especially where the meeting is to be held on short notice (see below, Chapter 9). Accordingly, it is usual to amend reg 62 to permit proxies to be lodged one hour before the meeting.
- If only one director is to be appointed, or a maximum number of directors is to be specified, reg 64 will need to be amended.
- Although reg 72 gives the directors power to delegate any or all of their powers to a committee, it may be necessary to extend the regulation to permit non-directors to be members of such committees. In such cases, it is usual to limit non-directors to less than half the committee and not permit such a committee to pass resolution unless a majority of directors vote in its favour.
- Regulations 73–80 contain provision for one-third of all directors to retire from office at each AGM, and such a requirement is often inappropriate for small companies and should be excluded. It should be noted that this provision must be excluded where it is intended

to dispense with AGMs by an elective resolution (see below, Chapter 10).
- It is often helpful to include an article to allow for the holding of board and general meetings by telephone, so that all parties do not have to be physically present in order for the meeting to be held.
- Regulation 81 specifies the circumstances in which a director may be removed from office. If it is intended to remove a director other than for one of the reasons set out in the regulation, there are a number of procedural difficulties (see below, Chapter 8) and, accordingly, the articles may provide for a director to be removed by a notice signed by all his co-directors (being at least two in number).
- Regulation 82 provides for the ordinary remuneration of the directors to be set by ordinary resolution. This regulation is sometimes extended to permit the directors to pay a director extra remuneration if he performs additional duties.
- Regulation 89 provides that a quorum for board meetings is to be determined by the directors and until so determined will be two. This will need to be amended to one where there is to be a sole director.
- Regulation 94 contains restrictions upon the circumstances in which a director with a conflict of interest is able to vote upon a particular resolution or be counted in the quorum of a particular board meeting. Depending upon the circumstances, it may be appropriate to exclude these restrictions and permit the directors a greater degree of flexibility (see below, 8.5).
- In circumstances where the company is to be a wholly owned subsidiary of another company, it may be helpful to include an 'overriding article' permitting the parent company to appoint and remove directors or to restrict their powers by notice delivered to the company.

Note: it is not necessary to amend the quorum provisions for general meetings contained in reg 40 where there is only one member, because s 370A expressly overrides the articles in such a case and provides for a quorum of one.

6.3   Use of information technology by companies

The Companies Act 1985 (Electronic Communications) Order 2000 (the Order) and the related *Guide to Recommended Best Practice,* produced by the Institute of Chartered Secretaries and Administrators (the Guide), have paved the way for companies to amend their articles. Notwithstanding that the Order stipulates that companies may take advantage of its provisions regardless of any provision to the contrary, or whether the articles are silent on the matter, the Guide recognises that many companies may wish to change their articles in order to avoid confusion. It therefore includes a best practice recommendation that companies should take steps to amend their articles specifically to facilitate the use of electronic communications as soon as is practicable. The following are examples of amendments typically made by companies to their articles:

- notices of shareholder meetings can be sent by email (see below for discussion with regard to AGMs);
- notices of directors' meetings can be sent by email;
- voting on a poll can be done electronically;
- a proxy can be appointed by email;
- board meetings can take place via a series of videoconferences or telephone calls, or via 'similar equipment' designed to allow everyone to take part in the meeting;
- a company can deliver any offer, notice or other document (including a share certificate) to a shareholder by email; and
- a notice or document sent by email can be treated as being delivered at the expiration of a set period from the time on the day it was sent.

The Order has also clarified previous uncertainties in the law as to whether AGM notices could be sent via email. Section 370 of the Act allows companies to provide in their articles the manner in which notice of meetings should be given. The Order amends regs 111 and 112 of Table A to allow the electronic communication (which includes fax and email) of AGM notices. Prior to the implementation of the Order, companies tended not to give notice via email because 'copies' of the report and accounts still had to be sent to shareholders under s 238. Reference to 'copies' of the report and accounts in s 238 was conservatively construed as meaning hard copies, since there was no provision in the Act specifically enabling delivery in non-physical form. Regulation 12 of the Order, however, amends s 238 to allow any document which the Act requires a company to submit physically to members to be sent, where the individual member agrees, to a fax number or email address. The Order also permits companies to place any communication on a website and, again where the member agrees, to send a notice of the availability to the member's email address. The changes made by the Order should enable companies to make significant cost savings in the distribution of documents to shareholders.

Whilst it is now relatively common practice to make provisions in a company's articles for board meetings to be conducted by telephone conference call or by video link, there is still debate as to whether board meetings could properly be held by email. It is arguable that email enables each director to contribute and to be aware of the other directors' contributions to the meeting. A court may therefore be prepared to accept this as a valid meeting, although there is no conclusive English authority on this issue. While it is sensible to ensure that articles are flexible, few companies have gone further than holding board meetings by telephonic communication notwithstanding that they have included provision in the articles to allow the conduct of board meetings by email. Similarly, although it would be theoretically possible for notice to be served on a company's directors by voicemail or by email, there is an increased risk of a director who failed to receive the message claiming that notice had not been properly served and the meeting therefore not properly convened. The articles of association generally include provisions for deemed receipt of any written notice but, to date, companies have not been prepared to extend such provisions to voicemail and email.

6.4 The articles as a contract

Section 14 provides that the memorandum and articles of association bind the company and its members to the same extent as if they respectively had been signed and sealed by each member and contained covenants on the part of each member to observe all the provisions of the memorandum and articles. Accordingly a member may, *prima facie*, enforce the articles against the company (or vice versa) or against another member.

Although the articles constitute a contract between the company and its members, there are a number of differences from a normal contract:

- the articles can be varied by a special resolution (see below, 6.6);
- there is no remedy of rectification if the articles are incorrectly registered, and it is probable that a member will be unable to recover damages against a company, since this would, in effect, result in a return of capital, which is generally prohibited (see below, Chapter 7).

In addition, it appears that whether a member can enforce a provision contained in the articles will depend on the capacity in which he sues. The general rule is that a member can only enforce those articles that confer rights upon him in his capacity as a shareholder (*Hickman v Kent or Romney Marsh Sheep Breeders' Association* [1915] 1 Ch 881). Accordingly, in *Eley v Positive Government Security Life Assurance Co* (1876) 1 Ex D 88, the plaintiff was unable to enforce a provision in the articles which appointed him as the company's solicitor for life, since that right was not conferred upon him in his capacity as a member. Although the House of Lords in *Salmon v Quinn and Axtens* [1909] AC 442 came to a different conclusion, it appears to be generally accepted that it is difficult for shareholders to enforce provisions in the articles which are conferred upon them other than in their capacity as shareholders. Accordingly, if a shareholder wishes to contract with the company in an alternative capacity, the terms of the agreement should be incorporated in a separate contract, which the shareholder will be able to enforce under normal contractual principles.

6.5 Relationship between the board and the general meeting

The division of power between the board and the general meeting depends entirely on the construction of the articles and, where power of management is delegated to the board, the shareholders, through a general meeting, are unable to interfere. Regulation 70 provides that:

> ... subject to the provisions of the Act, the memorandum and the articles and to any directions given by special resolution, the business of the company shall be managed by the directors who may exercise all the powers of the company.

Accordingly, the shareholders are only able to intervene in the management of the company where a special resolution can be passed. It is always open to the shareholders to remove the directors by ordinary resolution if they are unhappy with the management of the company (s 303 and see below, 8.4.4).

6.6 Alteration of the articles

The articles of a company may be changed, whatever the articles themselves say, by a special resolution (s 9(1)). If it is intended to entrench a provision, it is necessary to incorporate it in the memorandum. If the alteration of the articles would result in a variation of class rights, then additional formalities, such as a meeting of the relevant class of shareholders, may be necessary before the articles can be amended (see below, 7.6).

In the past, it seemed that a company could by contract agree not to alter its articles, although, in such a case, it was thought that a third party could only claim damages for breach and could not enforce the contract by specific performance nor obtain an injunction, since to do so would be inconsistent with the statutory power to alter articles. In *Russell v Northern Bank Development Corp Ltd* [1992] 1 WLR 588, the House of Lords rejected this principle. In that case, the court held that an agreement between a company and its shareholders not to issue further shares unless the consent of those shareholders was obtained, which therefore had the effect of restricting the alteration of the capital clause in the memorandum, constituted an unlawful fetter on the statutory power of the company to increase its share capital by ordinary resolution. Accordingly, a company now does not have power to enter into such undertakings. This principle will apply to all statutory powers contained in the Act – for example, the power of the company to alter its name by special resolution – and any agreement with the company, whether in the articles themselves or by contract, to restrict these statutory powers will be invalid. However, in *Russell,* the House of Lords accepted that shareholders were able to agree between themselves the manner in which their voting rights could be exercised and, therefore, an agreement between shareholders not to vote in favour of a resolution to increase capital would, for example, be valid.

Generally, a shareholder can vote in any manner that he wishes on a particular resolution. However, in relation to any amendment to the articles, a shareholder must vote *bona fide* in the best interests of the company as a whole (*Allen v Gold Reefs of West Africa* [1900] 1 Ch 656). There has been a good deal of judicial uncertainty as to the precise meaning of the test and whether it is of a subjective nature, based on a shareholder's belief, or whether it had to be referred to an objective standard. Its latest formulation is contained in *Greenhalgh v Arderne Cinemas Ltd* [1951] Ch 286 and is an odd combination of the two approaches. It was held that the phrase 'company as a whole' was taken to mean the company as a commercial entity distinct from its shareholders, and the case had to be taken of an individual hypothetical member and the question asked whether the resolution to amend the articles is, in the honest opinion of those who voted in its favour, for that person's benefit. The test is virtually impossible to apply in practice, since the answer will depend on whether the hypothetical member is assumed to be a shareholder who supports the amendment or one who objects to it.

There is a heavy burden of proof on the party alleging that the special resolution amending the articles should be set aside (akin, it was said in one case, to the grounds on which an appellate court would quash the verdict of a jury). The courts will be influenced in determining whether a resolution ought to be set aside by evidence of malice or discrimination by the majority in passing the relevant resolution.

7 Share Capital and Dividends

7.1 Types of share capital

There is almost no limit to the rights that can be attached to shares. The following list the main types of share capital often found in practice:

- Ordinary shares have the general right to vote and a residual right to receive dividends and any surplus of assets over liabilities on a winding-up. The rights of ordinary shareholders will depend on the rights attaching to other classes of shares. For example, if there are preference shares, ordinary shareholders will be entitled to receive dividends or any surplus on a winding-up after the preference shareholders.
- Preference shares give the holder a preferential right to receive a dividend and/or a share in a surplus on a winding-up in priority to ordinary shareholders. A preference share will normally entitle the holder to a fixed amount of dividend, usually expressed as a percentage of the nominal amount of the share. Furthermore, if the rights attaching to the share require that if a dividend is unable to be paid in any particular year it will be aggregated to the following year's entitlement, then the share is known as a cumulative preference share. Preference shares do not, normally, entitle the holder to vote unless the dividend payable on them are in arrears or the nature of the resolution affects the rights of the preference shareholder. Preference shares are normally used for institutional investors who want a fixed rate of return on their investment in a company.
- Deferred shares give the holder the right to receive dividends and/or a share of the surplus on a winding-up after preference and ordinary shareholders. Deferred shares are usually used for tax reasons.

In addition, these classes of shares may have other rights attached to them, for example:

- Shares may be redeemable and so entitle or require the holder to have his shares redeemed by the company in the circumstances permitted by the Act (see below, 7.7). Redeemable shares enable a member to withdraw his capital at a predetermined time without the need to liquidate the company.
- Shares may be convertible and so entitle or require the holder to convert his shares into those of another class at a predetermined time. Usually, the convertible share will be a form of preference share which is convertible into ordinary shares and the right of conversion may be triggered, for example, to enable the director/shareholder to obtain a greater stake in the company's equity as a reward for the company's improved financial performance.

7.2 Authority to issue shares

Section 80 prohibits the directors from allotting 'relevant securities' unless authority has been given to them by ordinary resolution or pursuant to the articles. Accordingly, the shareholders have some control over the issue of shares (see, also, below, 7.3). Failure to comply with the requirements of s 80 will render the directors liable to a fine, although the validity of the issue will not be affected even if the third party was aware of the directors' lack of authority.

Relevant securities are defined as meaning all shares in a particular company (other than subscriber shares or shares allotted pursuant to an employee share option scheme (as defined in s 743)) together with the right to subscribe for, or to convert any security into, shares in the company (s 80(2)). Accordingly, for example, appropriate authority would have to be obtained for the issue of loan stock which was convertible into ordinary shares. Allotment is defined as the unconditional right for a person to be included in the company's register of members in respect of shares (s 738).

The authority for the allotment of shares, whether contained in an ordinary resolution or the articles, must contain the following information:
- the maximum amount of relevant securities that may be allotted under the authority;
- whether the authority is unconditional or subject to conditions;
- the date on which the authority is to expire, which must not (unless an appropriate elective resolution has been passed (see below, Chapter 10)) exceed five years from the date of the appropriate resolution or, if the authorisation is contained in the articles, five years from the date of incorporation.

In addition, it may be advisable to include the following matters in the appropriate resolution:
- a statement authorising the directors to allot relevant securities after the authority has expired, provided that such shares are allotted pursuant to a contract entered into by the company prior to the expiry of the authority as permitted by s 80(7);
- where the authority is being renewed and the previous authority has not yet expired, a statement that the new authority replaces the existing authority, in order to avoid any possible confusion.

The authority can only be given over the current authorised share capital of a company and, accordingly, if the share capital is increased, it will be necessary to obtain a new authority in respect of the increased amount. Subject to that, the authority may be given for a particular issue or generally and may be subject to such conditions as are thought appropriate.

The authority may be varied, revoked or renewed by ordinary resolution notwithstanding that the authority is contained in the articles. If the authority is renewed, then it must contain the same information as required for the original authority. Any ordinary resolution giving or renewing an authority under s 80 must be filed with Companies House within 15 days of it being passed (s 380(4)(f)).

7.3 Pre-emption provisions

Generally speaking, s 89 prohibits the directors allotting 'equity securities' for cash unless the same or a more favourable offer is made to all shareholders in proportion to their holding of relevant shares in the company. The principle behind the section is to ensure that unless shareholder approval is obtained, any issue of shares will not dilute the proportion of shares held by existing shareholders. Failure to comply with the terms of the section will render those officers who knew of or authorised the contravention liable to a fine and such persons will be jointly and severally liable to compensate any person to whom an offer should have been made under s 89 for any damage or loss suffered (s 92). However, the allotment itself is valid and is not subject to challenge.

Equity securities are defined in s 94 as meaning relevant shares other than subscriber shares and bonus shares. Relevant shares are defined as meaning all shares in a company other than those that:
- as respects dividends and capital carry a right to participate only up to specified amount in a distribution, that is, preference shares;

- are held by or are to be allotted to a person in pursuance of an employees' share scheme (as defined by s 743).

Included in the definition of 'equity securities' is the grant of rights to subscribe for, or convert securities into, relevant shares. Accordingly, a preference share which is convertible into an ordinary share would be included in the definition.

The section sets out detailed requirements for the manner in which the offer is to be made to shareholders, how shareholders are to be notified of the offer and a minimum period of 21 days during which the offer is required to be kept open. These detailed requirements make compliance with the section rather onerous and, accordingly, many private companies take advantage of the power contained in s 91 to exclude the requirements of s 89 in their articles and adopt their own form of pre-emption provisions. Alternatively, the provisions of s 89 are able to be disapplied by special resolution in respect of allotments made by the directors pursuant to a general power under s 80 or in respect of a particular allotment of shares. Where the special resolution relates to the disapplication of s 89 in relation to a particular allotment, the directors must recommend the resolution to shareholders and circulate to them with the notice of meeting a statement explaining the reasons for their recommendation, the amount to be paid to the company in respect of the shares to be allotted and the directors' justification of the amount (s 95(5)).

The section is not applicable where the company is proposing to allot equity securities other than for cash and, therefore, the pre-emption provisions are not applicable where a company is, for example, allotting shares in consideration for the acquisition of assets or the shares of another company.

7.4 Issue of shares at a premium or a discount

Shares may be issued at a price that exceeds their par value provided that the requirements of the Act are complied with. Section 130 requires that the value of the premium over par value is transferred to the 'share premium account' which is required to be established in the company's accounts. This account is to be treated as if it was share capital (and therefore only able to be returned to members in restricted circumstances), save that it may be used in:

- paying up unissued shares to be allotted to members as fully paid bonus shares;

- writing off the company's preliminary expenses or the expenses of, or the commission paid or discount allowed on, any issue of shares or debentures;
- providing for the premium payable on redemption of debentures of the company.

No share premium account is required to be established ('merger relief') in those circumstances where a company issues shares at a premium as consideration for acquiring at least 90% of the shares of another company, or where shares are allotted to companies in the same group and the requirements of ss 131 and 132, respectively, are fulfilled.

Shares are not permitted to be issued at a discount to their par value. If shares are so allotted to a member, that member is liable to pay to the company the amount of the discount together with interest (s 100).

7.5 Financial assistance

Where a person is proposing to acquire or has acquired shares in a company, it is not lawful for the company or its subsidiaries to give financial assistance directly or indirectly for the purpose of the acquisition or reducing any liability incurred by that person for the purpose of the acquisition (s 151). Breach of the section is a criminal offence and the company and every officer in default will be liable to a fine. A transaction in breach of s 151 will also be *ultra vires* the company and, therefore, unenforceable.

Financial assistance is not, itself, defined in the Act, although s 152 specifies the manner in which the assistance may be given. Financial assistance may be by way of gift, guarantee, security or indemnity, loan or 'any other financial assistance given by a company the net assets of which are thereby reduced or which has no net assets'. Common examples of financial assistance which are *prima facie* prohibited by the Act are:

- where a company lends money to a person for the purpose of acquiring its own shares;
- where a company pays shareholders' legal and accounting fees incurred in acquiring the company;
- where the assets of a company are charged to secure a loan which has been taken out by the new shareholders to finance the acquisition.

Whether a particular activity constitutes financial assistance is often one of the most difficult questions to determine in practice. Care should be taken to analyse the activities of the company prior to and post its acquisition to determine whether the provisions of s 151 are breached. It should be noted that financial assistance given by a foreign incorporated company to its UK parent does not fall within the ambit of s 151, despite the express wording of the statute (*Arab Bank plc v Mercantile Holdings Ltd* [1994] Ch 71).

There are a number of important exceptions to s 151 which permit a company, where it would otherwise constitute financial assistance, to:

- pay a dividend;
- allot bonus shares;
- reduce its share capital where the approval of the court has been obtained;
- redeem or purchase its own shares.

In addition, there are a number of other exceptions which restrict the application of s 151 in relation to schemes of arrangement or reconstructions pursuant to s 425, s 110 of the Insolvency Act 1986, Pt I of the Insolvency Act 1986, in connection with the provision of finance to employee share option schemes (as defined in s 743) or enabling shares to be held by employees (s 153(4)).

A further exception to s 151 is where the company's principal purpose in giving the assistance is not to give it for the purpose of the acquisition, or the giving of the assistance for that purpose is but an incidental part of some larger purpose of the company and, in both cases, the assistance is given in good faith (s 153(1)). This exception has been substantially restricted in its ambit by *Brady v Brady* [1989] AC 755, which held that the exception had to be construed narrowly in view of the mischief at which s 151 was aimed and the danger that a wide application would deprive s 151 of any real meaning. In that case, the reason why the company entered into the financial assistance was to enable part of a group of companies to be sold to a shareholder in order to avoid management deadlock. The House of Lords held that this did not fall within the exception specified in s 153(1), since the only purpose of the financial assistance was to allow the shares to be acquired and the commercial advantages flowing from the financing were a by-product rather than an independent purpose. It was necessary to distinguish between a purpose and the reason why a purpose was formed.

The most important exception for private companies is that they are able to give financial assistance, provided that: (a) net assets are not reduced (for example, where the company gives a guarantee) or, where net assets are reduced, the assistance is given out of distributable profits;

and (b) the requirements of ss 155 and 156 are fulfilled. These requirements are:

- A statutory declaration has to be made by all the company's directors which sets out the nature of the financial assistance, the business of the company and the identity of the person to receive the financial assistance. The declaration is required to state that the directors have formed the opinion that, immediately after the giving of the assistance, the company will be able to pay its debts as they fall due during the year immediately following the making of the declaration. If it is intended to wind up the company within 12 months, the declaration has to state that the company will pay its debts in full within 12 months of the commencement of the winding-up.
- The statutory declaration has to have affixed to it a report from the auditors confirming that, having made appropriate investigations, the opinion of the directors is not unreasonable.
- A special resolution has to be passed approving the financial assistance and must be passed within a week of the directors making the statutory declaration. At the meeting, the declaration and auditors' report must be available for inspection. (A resolution is not necessary if the company giving the financial assistance is a wholly owned subsidiary.)
- The statutory declaration, auditor's report and special resolution have to be filed with Companies House within 15 days of the resolution being passed or, if no special resolution is required, within 15 days of the declaration being made. Power is given to shareholders holding 10% or more in nominal value of the company's shares or any class thereof to apply to the court for cancellation of the resolution. Where authorisation has been obtained for the company to give financial assistance, the assistance must not be given within four weeks of the date that the special resolution is passed (so allowing an application to be made to the court) unless all members voted in favour of the resolution. The financial assistance is not permitted to be made after the expiry of eight weeks from the date of the statutory declaration (s 158).

The courts seem to take a reasonably relaxed approach to the manner in which the procedural obligations need to be fulfilled, presumably because to do otherwise would result in the financial assistance being unlawful. For example, in *Re NL Electrical Ltd, Ghosh and another v 3i plc* [1994] 1 BCLC 22, the company failed to use the correct prescribed form to make the directors' statutory declaration required by s 155(6) and failed to deliver the statutory declaration within the 15 day period. The court held that, nevertheless, the financial assistance had been validly given. The obligation related to the contents of the particulars and not the particular layout of the form, and, since all the appropriate information had been given, it was not relevant which form was used. With regard to late delivery, s 156 provides for a penalty, and it followed that this was the only consequence of late delivery. Similarly, in *Re S H & Co (Realisation) 1990 Ltd* [1993] BCC 60, the court held that proper particulars had been given notwithstanding that they did not contain details of the property charged, the nature of the charge or the fact that a guarantee had been given.

The DTI is currently reviewing the need for reforming the financial assistance rules given the current uncertainty arising from the *Brady* decision and the all encompassing nature of the legislation which results in many 'innocent' cases of financial assistance being caught.

7.6 Class rights

If the share capital of a company is divided into different classes, the Act restricts the ability of a company to vary those rights.

Class rights are those rights that attach to shares and include the rights to vote, to receive a dividend and a share of the surplus on a winding-up. For example, if a further class of preference shares were to be issued which ranked ahead of the existing preference shares for the purposes of dividends, this would amount to a variation of the existing preference shareholder rights. However, the variation must be to the rights themselves and not merely be diminishing the value or enjoyment of those rights. Accordingly, for example, in absence of anything to the contrary in the memorandum or articles, no class consent is necessary for issuing additional shares of an existing class, even if this would result in a change of control of the company (see *White v Bristol Aeroplane Co Ltd* [1953] Ch 65). The Act itself provides that any alteration of a provision contained in the company's articles for the variation of rights attached to shares or the insertion of any such procedure is to be treated as a variation of class rights (s 125(7)).

The meaning of 'class rights' was extended in *Cumbrian Newspapers Group Ltd v Cumberland and Westmorland Herald Newspaper and Printing Co Ltd* [1987] Ch 1 to cover rights or benefits that, although not attached to any particular shares, were conferred on a shareholder in his capacity as shareholder. In that case, it was held that the right of pre-emption and the right to appoint a director were class rights.

The procedure for variation of class rights contained in s 125 depends on whether the rights are contained in the memorandum or articles and whether there is any procedure for variation contained in the memorandum or articles. Table I (see below, p 61) sets out the principal requirements contained in the Act.

The provisions set out in the Act relating to holding of meetings (see Chapter 9) apply, in absence of specific provision in the Articles, equally to class meetings save that:
- quorums at class meetings shall be two persons present in person or by proxy, holding at least one-third in nominal value of issued shares of the relevant class and at an adjourned meeting one person or a proxy holding shares of the relevant class;
- any holder of shares of the relevant class present in person or by proxy may demand a poll (s 125(6)).

Where class rights have been varied in accordance with the requirement of the Act or the memorandum and articles of association, holders of not less than 15% of shares of the relevant class (who did not consent to or vote in favour of the resolution) may apply to the court to have the variation cancelled within 21 days of the relevant consent or resolution being passed (s 127). The court is able, if it believes the variation to be unfairly prejudicial to the applicant, to cancel the variation.

7.7 Redemption of shares

A limited company may, provided that its articles so permit, issue shares which are to be redeemed by or at the option of the company or the shareholder. Table A includes provision for a company to issue redeemable shares (reg 3).

It is now certain that s 133 of the Companies Act 1989, which contains specific provisions as to the terms and manner of redemption of shares, will not come in to force. Consultation on the provision, which required that the terms and conditions of redemption (particularly the date of, and the amount payable on, redemption) be set out in the articles of the company, produced an overwhelmingly negative response and the DTI now has no intention of bringing s 133 into force.

As the law stands, the articles do not need to make any special provision relating to redemption of shares.

Redeemable shares may only be redeemed if they have been fully paid.

The Act specifies the funds that can be used in order to effect the redemption. The general rule is that the nominal value of the shares can be redeemed out of distributable profits or the proceeds of the fresh issue of shares. Where the shares that are to be redeemed were issued at par, any premium payable on redemption must be out of distributable profits. If the shares were issued at a premium, then the proceeds of a fresh issue of shares can be used to fund the payment by the company of the premium to the extent of the aggregate of the premium received by the company or the amount of share premium account, whichever is the smaller (s 160(2)). Accordingly, if the share premium account has been reduced in a manner permitted by the Act (see above, 7.4), this will, proportionately, reduce the ability of the company to finance that part of the purchase price representing the premium originally paid on the shares by way of a fresh issue of shares.

In limited circumstances, a private company may redeem shares out of capital (see below, 7.8).

Shares that are redeemed are cancelled but the authorised capital remains the same, so that additional shares equivalent to the nominal value of the shares redeemed are available for issue without increasing the authorised share capital (s 160(4)).

Table I

Document where class rights are contained	Document where procedure for variation of rights is contained	Requirements for variation
1 Memorandum	None	All members of the company must agree to variation (s 125(5)) or scheme of arrangement made pursuant to s 425
2 Memorandum	Express prohibition in memorandum on variation of class rights	No variation permitted (s17) unless scheme of arrangement made pursuant to s 425
3 Memorandum or otherwise	Memorandum or articles	(a) If variation of rights is in connection with: (i) the giving, variation, revocation or renewal of an authority for allotment under s 80; or (ii) reduction of share capital pursuant to s 135, then either: (i) holders of 3/4 in nominal value of the relevant class consent in writing; or (ii) an extraordinary resolution passed at class meeting and any additional requirements of the memorandum and articles are complied with (s 125(3)) (b) If variation is otherwise than in connection with the matters stated in (a) and variation provisions are contained in the memorandum, the requirements contained therein must be fulfilled
4 Memorandum	Articles at time of incorporation	Provided that reason for variation of class rights is not connected with the reasons set out in para 3(a) above, rights can be varied in accordance with the provisions of the articles (s 125(4))
5 Otherwise than in memorandum	Articles (whether or not included at time of incorporation)	
6 Otherwise than in memorandum	None	Either: (i) holders of 3/4 nominal value relevant class consent in writing; or (ii) extraordinary resolution passed at class meeting and any additional requirement of the memorandum and articles are complied with (s 125(2))

7.8 Purchase of a company's own shares

A limited company may, provided that its articles so permit, purchase its own shares. Table A includes provision for a company to purchase its own shares (reg 35).

A company may wish to purchase its own shares to remove a difficult shareholder or to help a shareholder where he needs to sell some shares and where no other shareholder can afford to buy them.

The procedure for a limited company to purchase its own shares is as follows:

- A contract is prepared for the purchase (but not yet signed by the company).
- A general meeting has to be convened proposing a special resolution approving the proposed contract (s 164(2)).
- The contract must be on display at the company's registered office for 15 days before the meeting is held and therefore the meeting cannot be held on shorter notice than this, although a written resolution can, if required, be used (see below, Chapter 10).
- The contract must be on display at the meeting itself (s 164(6)).
- At the meeting, any shareholder whose votes are to be repurchased may not vote: if he does vote his votes are not to be counted (s 164(5)).
- Once the resolution is passed, the company is able to sign the contract and title to the shares is transferred to the company by a stock transfer form.
- Stamp duty is not paid on the stock transfer form but the company is required to complete and file Form 169 within 28 days of the purchase by the company, which is stamped at 0.5% of the consideration paid (s 169).
- The contract is required to be kept at the registered office of the company for 10 years and be available for inspection by members (s 169(4) and (5)).

The authority may be renewed, varied or revoked by special resolution and, to the extent necessary, the procedure set out above is followed. As with a redemption of shares, on purchase the shares are cancelled but the authorised capital remains the same, so that additional shares equivalent to the nominal value of the shares purchased are available for issue without increasing the authorised capital (s 162(2)).

A company is able to purchase its shares out of distributable profits (as defined by s 263(2)) or a fresh issue of shares, and the same rules relating to the funds which can be used for the repurchase apply in the same manner as are applicable to a company's redemption of shares (s 162(2); see above, 7.7). In addition, a private limited company is able, provided that its articles so permit (see, for example, reg 35 of Table A), to purchase shares out of capital (s 171). Purchases out of capital are only permitted to the extent that the purchase price exceeds available profits (calculated in accordance with s 172) and the proceeds of any new issue made for the purpose of the purchase. Accordingly, purchases out of capital are only permitted as a last resort.

The following procedure, set out in ss 173–75, has to be carried out in order for a company to make a purchase or redemption out of capital:

- The directors have to make a statutory declaration on Form 173, specifying the amount of capital to be used in the purchase and stating that, immediately after the payment of capital, the company will be able to pay its debts and be able to do so for the year immediately thereafter and that the company will be able to continue to carry on its business as a going concern throughout that year.
- The statutory declaration has to have affixed to it a report from the auditors confirming that the opinion of the directors is not unreasonable and that the amount of capital used is permitted by the Act.
- A general meeting has to be convened proposing a special resolution to authorise the payment. The resolution has to be passed within the week immediately following the making of the declaration by the directors and the declaration and auditors' report has to be available for inspection at the meeting.
- Within one week of the passing of the resolution, the company must publish a notice giving details of the purchase: (a) in the *London Gazette* if the company is registered in England and Wales or in the *Edinburgh Gazette* if the company is registered in Scotland; and (b) in a national newspaper. Alternatively, the notice is given individually to each creditor.
- Not later than the publication or distribution of the notice to the creditors, the statutory declaration and auditors' report must be filed with Companies House and be kept at the registered office on display to the public for a period of five weeks from the date of the passing of the appropriate resolution.

For a period of five weeks from the date of the resolution, any non-consenting member or creditor can apply to the court for relief. The court is able to cancel the terms of the resolution. Within two weeks of the expiry of the five week period, the company is able to make the payment for its shares out of capital.

7.9 Alteration of share capital

7.9.1 Increase, division and consolidation of share capital

If the issued share capital is less than the authorised share capital, the capital can be increased by the issue of additional shares without need to amend the articles. The authorities that the directors are required to have in order to make an issue of shares are set out above, 7.2 and 7.3. An increase in the authorised share capital can be made by ordinary resolution provided that the articles so allow (s 121 and see reg 32 of Table A). Notice of any increase of share capital must be made to Companies House within 15 days of the passing of the resolution on Form 123. Provided that power is taken in the articles, the Act permits, by the passing of an ordinary resolution, share capital to be subdivided into smaller units (for example, each £1 share is converted into two 50 p shares) or consolidated into larger amounts (for example, two 50 p shares being converted in a £1 share) (s 121(2)).

7.9.2 Reduction of share capital

A company may (other than in the circumstances outlined in this chapter) only reduce its issued share capital if it is authorised in its articles, a special resolution is passed and the reduction is approved by the court. A company may wish to reduce its capital for any number of reasons, some of which are outlined in s 135, such as because it has been trading badly and the share capital is no longer represented by its assets or the capital is in excess to its requirements. The court, in determining whether to confirm the reduction, will attempt to ensure that the interests of creditors will not be prejudiced and the reduction does not unfairly discriminate between different classes of shares. The detailed requirements are set out in ss 135–41.

7.10 Dividends

7.10.1 When a dividend can be paid

A company can only pay a dividend if it has 'profits available for the purpose' (s 263(1)). Section 263(3) provides that a company's distributable profits are its accumulated, realised profits (so far as not previously utilised by distribution or capitalisation) less its accumulated, realised losses (so far as not previously written off in a reduction or reorganisation of capital). Realised profit means such profits as fall to be treated as such in accordance with generally accepted accounting principles (s 262(3)).

Calculations of the distributable profits must be based on the 'relevant accounts'. These will be the company's last audited annual accounts, except in two situations as provided for in s 270(4), namely:

(a) where the distribution would contravene the relevant section if reference was made only to the company's last annual accounts, that is, the last annual accounts do not show sufficient distributable profit but the company has subsequently traded profitably. In such a case, interim accounts become the relevant accounts on which to base the calculation of distributable profits and any dividend paid will be termed an 'interim dividend' (see below, 7.10.2). Unlike the situation where the last annual accounts are relied on, if interim accounts are used there is no requirement for the accounts to be accompanied by an auditors' report, although it must comply with the requirements of s 272;

(b) where the distribution is proposed to be declared during the company's first accounting reference period, or before any accounts are laid before shareholders in respect of that period. In this case, initial accounts must be drawn up and be audited by the company's auditors and otherwise comply with the requirements of s 273.

Alongside the statutory requirement that the company must have sufficient distributable profits, directors are also under a common law duty to consider whether the dividend payment is in the best interests of the company.

A dividend is not payable until declared by the company or, in the case of an interim dividend, the directors, unless the company's articles provide for automatic payment of a dividend once there are sufficient distributable profits.

7.10.2 Final and interim dividends

An interim dividend is one that is paid between two AGMs, whereas a final dividend is declared at an annual meeting. A company's articles usually allow for the declaration of a final dividend by the passing of an ordinary resolution in a general meeting, provided that the dividend shall not exceed the amount recommended by directors (see reg 102). Interim dividends, however, may be declared and paid by directors without recourse to a general meeting if the articles gives them the power to do so. The shareholders cannot require the directors to declare an interim dividend (*Scott v Scott* [1943] 1 All ER 582). Before declaring an interim dividend, the directors should be satisfied that the financial position of the company warrants the payment of such a dividend from distributable profits (*Lucas v Fitzgerald* (1903) 20 TLR 16, p 18). The case of *Re City Equitable Fire Insurance Co Ltd* [1925] Ch 407 suggests that directors should not rely solely on the auditors' opinion but must themselves make an informed assessment as to the value of the company's assets and liabilities.

Once a final dividend has been declared, it cannot be revoked or reduced in value but is deemed to be a debt to the shareholders. In contrast, the decision to pay an interim dividend can be varied or rescinded up until the time when the dividend is to be paid (*Lagunas Nitrate Co v Schroeder & Co and Schmidt* (1901) 85 LT 22).

7.10.3 Equality of treatment of shareholders

In the absence of any contrary provision in the company's articles, dividends must be paid proportionately to the nominal value of the shares rather than to their paid up value. It should be noted, however, that Table A provides for dividend payments to be proportionate to the amounts that have been paid up on shares from time to time during the period for which the dividend is declared.

Furthermore, a dividend must be declared at the same rate for all shares of a particular class.

7.10.4 Method of payment of dividends

Dividends are paid to those who are registered on the company's register of members at the date on which the dividend is declared. For ease of administration, the company may close its register and refuse to register transfers of shares for a short period before the dividend is payable.

Unless the company's articles provide otherwise, a dividend must be paid in cash and the company can be prevented from paying in another manner (*Wood v Odessa Waterworks Co* (1889) 42 Ch 636). However, the articles commonly contain the power (for example, reg 105), upon the recommendation of the directors, to pay the dividend wholly or partly in a form other than cash.

7.10.5 Illegally paid dividends

A dividend is unlawful if:
- it is paid when the company had insufficient profits available for the purpose; or
- appropriate annual, initial or interim accounts were not prepared and, in the case of initial or interim accounts, such accounts have not been filed with Companies House; or
- in the case of annual or interim accounts, these were not accompanied by a report from the company's auditor, which satisfies s 271(4) or s 273(4).

The company has an action to recover the amount unlawfully paid against any of its directors who were aware, or who ought to have been aware, of the infringement of the statutory requirements. A claim will also lie against any members of the company who knew or who had reasonable grounds for believing that the dividend was being unlawfully paid (s 277).

7.10.6 Tax treatment of dividends

When a company pays a dividend, there is no longer a requirement to account for Advance Corporation Tax. Individual shareholders are entitled to a tax credit of one-ninth of the net dividend, which is equal to 10% of the aggregate of the dividend and the tax credit (the 'gross dividend'). Individual shareholders who are subject to tax at the lower or the basic rate will be subject to tax on the dividend at the rate of 10% of the gross dividend, but the tax credit will satisfy in full their tax liability so they will have no further tax to pay. Individual shareholders subject to higher rate income tax are subject to tax at 32.5% of the gross dividend, but can set off the amount of the tax credit against the amount of their tax liability. Non-taxpayers are unable to reclaim a refund of the tax credit.

8 Directors

8.1 Who can become a director

Any person (including another company or a minor) can become a director of a company, provided that he is not the subject of a disqualification order made by the court pursuant to the Company Directors Disqualification Act 1986 (see below, 8.10).

8.2 Types of directors

There is no helpful definition of a director in the Act. Section 741 provides that director includes any person occupying the position of director, by whatever name called. In essence, a director is a person who has been appointed as such in accordance with the articles and who is entitled to attend and vote at board meetings. There are a number of different types of directors:

- An executive director is a director who has a contract of employment with the company and who, as a consequence, is involved in its day to day management. A non-executive director does not have a service contract and usually takes a supervisory role over the executive management.
- A managing director is an executive director to whom the board has delegated some or all of their powers in accordance with the provision of the articles (see reg 72). In addition to a managing director, there may be other directors who the board has delegated specific power to, for example, a finance or sales director.
- An alternate director is a person appointed by a director, in accordance with the provisions of the articles, who is able to attend and vote at board meetings in place of the director who appointed him. For example, regs 65–69 provide for the appointment of any director or any other person approved by the directors as an alternate.

- A shadow director is a person in accordance with whose directions or instructions the directors of a company are accustomed to act, other than a person giving advice in a professional capacity (s 741 of the Act and s 251 of the Insolvency Act 1986). Certain specified sections of the Act and the Insolvency Act 1986 treat shadow directors in the same manner as if they were directors (for example, ss 309, 319, 320–22, 330–46 of the Act and s 214(7) of the Insolvency Act 1986).

Secretary of State for Trade and Industry v Deverell and Another [2000] 2 All ER 365 clarified the statutory definition of a shadow director by establishing the following principles:

- non-professional advice can come within the definition of 'direction and instructions'; advice, directions and instructions all share the common feature of 'guidance';
- the 'directions and instructions' which a shadow director gives need not extend to all (or even most) of the corporate activities of the company;
- a subservient role, or surrender of discretion by the properly appointed directors may be relevant but is not necessary for a finding of shadow directorship;
- a shadow director need not 'lurk in the shadows', although he might frequently do so.

It is not uncommon for a person to have a job title that includes the word 'director' even though he is not. In such a case, the employee will have ostensible authority to bind the company as if he was a director, provided that all the other conditions necessary for a third party to rely on such authority are fulfilled (see above, 5.6).

8.3 Appointment of directors

The first directors of the company are appointed at the time of incorporation (see above, Chapter 3). The manner in which additional directors are to be appointed will depend upon the terms of the articles. Table A gives the power of appointment to the shareholders in general meeting, although the directors are able to appoint a director on a temporary basis until the next AGM. In such a case, not less than seven nor more than 28 clear days' notice has to be given to shareholders of the person who is recommended by the directors for appointment at the relevant general meeting, unless the director is retiring by rotation (regs 77–79). As an alternative, the power to appoint directors could be given exclusively to the board.

8.4 Termination of director's office

8.4.1 Resignation

A director is able to resign his office at any time upon giving notice to the company, although, if he does so, he may be in breach of any service contract that he has with the company. One point to watch – where minutes are being drafted for a board meeting at which a director is to resign, ensure that the resignation of the director only takes effect from the conclusion of the meeting if it is necessary for the resigning director to be present for purposes of a quorum.

8.4.2 Retirement by rotation

Table A provides that at the first AGM all the directors are to retire from office and at subsequent meetings one-third (or the nearest multiple) of directors are to resign (reg 73). The object is to ensure that directors do not entrench themselves on the board without shareholder approval, but the provisions in Table A are subject to two important qualifications:

(a) executive directors are not subject to retirement by rotation (reg 84);
(b) any director who retires by rotation is able to be reappointed at the same general meeting (reg 80).

8.4.3 Disqualification of a director

Articles usually provide that a director will be disqualified in certain circumstances. Regulation 81 provides that a director is to vacate his office in the following circumstances:

- if he ceases to be a director by virtue of any provision of the Act (such as being removed in accordance with s 303; see below, 8.4.4) or is prohibited by law from being a director (such as under the Company Directors Disqualification Act 1986 (see below, 8.10));
- if he becomes bankrupt or makes arrangement or composition with his creditors;
- if he suffers from mental disorder and his affairs become subject to the jurisdiction of the court;
- if he is absent for a period of six months or more from meetings of directors and the directors resolve that his office be vacated.

8.4.4 Removal of a director

The articles may provide that a director can be removed by notice served upon him by all his co-directors, and this is an amendment which is commonly made to Table A (see above, 6.2).

The Act includes provision for shareholders to remove a director from his office by ordinary resolution notwithstanding any contrary provision in the articles or in any contract between the company and the director (s 303). There are certain points to note about the section:

- It is necessary that special notice be given of any resolution proposed under s 303. Accordingly, s 379 requires that intention to move the resolution is to be given to the company at least 28 days before the meeting is to be held. The directors, in convening the necessary meeting, must give members notice of the resolution at the same time as the notice of the meeting. There are no special requirements for the notice of the meeting, which can, accordingly, be held on 14 days' notice (unless the articles provide for a longer period). There is an anti-avoidance provision contained in the section which provides that, if the directors attempt to frustrate a member's proposal by calling a meeting within the 28 day period, the notice will be deemed to have been properly given.

- The company is required by s 304 to give notice of the intention to remove a director to the relevant director who is able to require the company to distribute to members' representations, unless such representations are of an unreasonable length or an attempt to 'secure needless publicity for defamatory matter'. The director is able to speak at the relevant meeting.

The removal of a director under this section is without prejudice to any right to damages he may have under a service contract with the company. Despite the clear intention of the legislature expressed in s 303 to prevent directors from entrenching themselves on the board by provision in the articles, it has been expressly recognised by the judiciary in *Bushell v Faith* [1970] AC 1099 that weighted voting rights can be attached to shares so as to enable the holder to defeat any resolution to remove him as a director.

It is possible to avoid the need for special notice by inserting a provision in the articles to permit shareholders to remove a director by means of special or extraordinary resolution. In such a case, although 21 or 14 days' notice of the meeting would need to be given, no special notice is required, nor does the director get rights to send a circular to shareholders or speak at the relevant meeting. Furthermore, the meeting can be held on short notice (see below, 9.3). However, a note of caution should be sounded – the use of this procedure may, if challenged in court, be viewed as an attempt to subvert the intention of Parliament. Although this risk is small, given the court's approach in *Bushell v Faith*, nevertheless there must still be a concern that this course of action would be subject to challenge.

8.5 Directors' fiduciary duties

A director owes certain duties to the company (not, generally, to its shareholders individually). In particular:

- A director must act *bona fide* in the best interests of the company at all times. Accordingly, this would preclude, for example, the director taking a decision which would profit himself or some third party at the expense of the company. The test as to whether a director has fulfilled this duty is subjective so that the court will only interfere where no reasonable director could have acted in a particular manner.
- A director must not place himself in a position where his own interests and those of the company may conflict. At common law, any contract entered into in breach of this duty is voidable at the instance of the company and the director will have to account for any profit made. The rule applies differently in respect of contracts entered into by a director and corporate opportunities acquired by him.
- Contracts – the strict rule has been modified in relation to contracts so that a director may be able to enter into a contract with the company and avoid accounting for any profit earned, provided that: (a) the articles permit him to do so; and (b) any disclosure requirements contained in the articles and the Act are followed.

  Table A permits directors to be interested in contracts and not to account for profits (reg 85) but they are not generally permitted to vote or be counted in the quorum of any board meeting which considers the relevant contract (regs 94 and 95). Often, an amendment is made to Table A to permit directors to vote and be counted in a quorum in such a situation.

- In addition, the provisions contained in s 317 have to be complied with. This section requires that a director who is directly or indirectly interested in a contract or proposed contract must disclose his interest to the board. Disclosure must be to the full board and not to one of its committees (*Guinness plc v Saunders* [1988] BCLC 607). However, even where formal compliance with s 317 was not made, a company will not be entitled to rescind the relevant contract if, as a matter of fact, all the other directors knew of the relevant interest (*Runciman v Walter Runciman* [1992] BCLC 1084). Failure to comply with the terms of the section renders the director concerned liable to a fine and any protection afforded by the articles will be lost. Although the situation is far from clear, breach of s 317 alone (that is, not in association with a breach of the common law rules) will not affect the validity of the contract. It should be stressed that observance with s 317 is purely negative in effect, so that compliance with it will not render a contract valid, which would otherwise be voidable if the articles do not contain a validating provision.

- Section 317 does permit a general disclosure to be made by a director of companies in which he or persons with whom he is connected (within the meaning of s 346) are shareholders which will constitute sufficient disclosure under this section in respect of contracts entered into by the company with such persons. A general disclosure of companies in which the director is also a director is not permitted and, accordingly, any contracts with such companies must be disclosed at each relevant board meeting. The disclosure should be a full and frank declaration of the precise nature of the interest that the director holds. It is important to note that, where there is a sole director, the courts consider that compliance with s 317 is required and, indeed, has an enhanced value since there are no other directors to witness or police his actions (*Neptune (Vehicle Washing Equipment) Ltd v Fitzgerald* [1995] 3 WLR 108). Accordingly, the written minutes of a 'meeting' of a sole director should include a disclosure of any relevant interest.

- Corporate opportunities – in the absence of anything to the contrary in the articles, the strict rule continues to apply (despite some recent antipodean authorities to the contrary) in respect of corporate opportunities (see *Regal (Hastings) Ltd v Gulliver* [1942] 1 All ER 378) so that a director may be called to account in respect of profits derived from an opportunity acquired in his capacity as a director. This rule applies notwithstanding that the company was unable to take advantage of the opportunity itself or that the director, in so doing, was acting in the best interests of the company. Accordingly, for a director to keep monies derived from such corporate opportunities, full disclosure must be made to shareholders and their approval obtained. It is difficult for shareholders to monitor the activities of the directors effectively and even more difficult for them to bring an action against the directors (see below, Chapter 12) and, therefore, it is thought that a strict rule is necessary to ensure that directors keep to the straight and narrow. This duty does not, however, automatically preclude a person from being a director of two or more companies, save that a director cannot use confidential information acquired in his capacity of a particular company for the benefit of another company of which he is also a director (*Bell v Lever Brothers* [1932] AC 161).

- A director is required to use the powers given to him for their proper and not for some collateral purpose. A director will be in breach of this duty even if he is acting in the best interests of the company in using the power improperly. For example, the power to issue shares is to be used to raise capital and not to defeat a takeover bid by putting shares in the hands of a person who would not accept the takeover offer (*Howard Smith Ltd v Ampol Petroleum Ltd* [1974] AC 821). In order to determine the proper purpose of any power, it is necessary to construe the relevant article in order to ascertain the nature of the power and the limits within which it may be exercised. It is then necessary to look at the substantive (as opposed to any incidental) purpose for which the power was exercised and reach an appropriate conclusion – usually easier said than done!

- A director cannot fetter his future discretion, and therefore he is unable, for example, to bind himself by contract as to how he will cast his votes at board meetings. However, it is possible for directors to enter into a contract which they believe to be in the best interests of the company even if the terms of the contract limit their discretion in the future and it binds them to exercise their powers in a particular manner which, at that time, is not necessarily in the best interests of the company (*Fulham Football Club v Cabra Estates* [1992] BCC 863).

8.6 Duties of care and skill

The traditional common law approach has been to require directors to exercise very little skill and care in the performance of his role. *Re Barings plc (No 5)* [1999] 1 BCLC 523 has reformulated the position on directors in the context of an application to disqualify a director under the Company Directors Disqualification Act 1986:

- Directors have, both collectively and individually, a continuing duty to acquire and maintain a sufficient knowledge and understanding of the company's business to enable them properly to discharge their duties as directors.

- Each individual director owes duties to the company to inform himself about its affairs and to join with his co-directors in supervising and controlling such affairs. Accordingly, whilst delegation of certain directors responsibilities is permitted, a director always has an obligation of control and supervision (*Re Westmid Packing Services Ltd* [1998] 2 All ER 124).

- A director's duty of care and skill is that expressed by the Court of Appeal of New South Wales in *Daniels v Anderson* (1995) 16 ACSR 607 (as cited with approval and adopted):

> A person who accepts the office of director of a particular company undertakes the responsibility of ensuring that he or she understands the nature of the duty a director is called upon to perform. That duty will vary according to the size and business of the particular company and the experience or skills that the director held himself or herself out to have in support of appointment to the office. None of this is novel. It turns upon the natural expectations and reliance placed by shareholders on the experience and skill of a particular director ... The duty includes that of acting collectively to manage the company.

The application of these general standards will depend on the facts of the case, but the following standards are relevant:

- the business of the company;
- the size of the company;
- the organisation of the company;
- the role assigned to/assumed by the director;
- the experience and skills the director has *or has held himself out as having*;
- the remuneration received by the director.

This case followed *Norman v Theodore Goddard* [1991] BCLC 1028 and *Re D'Jan of London Ltd* [1993] BCC 646, where the same judge in both cases suggested that the duty of care owed by a director at common law is accurately stated in s 214(4) of the Insolvency Act 1986. This section lays down an objective test of a reasonably diligent person having both (a) the general knowledge, skill and experience that may reasonably be expected of a person carrying out the same functions as are carried out by that director in relation to that company, and (b) the general knowledge, skill and experience that that director has.

More recently, in *Re Landhurst Leasing Ltd* [1999] 1 BCLC 286, where the question of the director's (in)competence on the basis of the test enunciated *in Re D'Jan* was considered, it was held that a junior director cannot put unquestioning faith in his superiors: '... their duties require them to act with independence and courage.' Accordingly:

- an employee who is promoted to the board cannot carry on as though nothing has changed;

- a director may have to discharge his duty by 'blowing the whistle' to the company's non-executive directors or auditors.

The common law duties referred to above are subject to the following important qualifications:

- Executive directors will have much higher duties of care and skill, which derive from their service contracts. Accordingly, such a director will have an obligation to perform his duties by reference to an objective standard, will be required to devote his full time to his duties and will not be able to delegate his duties unless expressly authorised to do so.
- The Insolvency Act 1986 has introduced a higher degree of skill and care on directors whose companies go into insolvent liquidation (see s 214 of that Act and above, 2.5).

8.7 Deals with directors

In addition to the restrictions placed upon a director contracting with the company at common law, there are a number of statutory provisions which relate to transactions between a director and his company. The following are relevant:

- Section 317 requires directors to notify their interest in contracts with the company to the board (see above, 8.5).
- Section 320 requires shareholders' approval where a company is selling to or buying from a director (or his close family or associated companies as defined in s 346) assets other than cash and the value of the transaction, being of a value of more than £2,000, exceeds the lower of £100,000 or 10% of the company's net assets. Failure to comply with the requirements of the section result in the transaction being voidable and the director having to account for any profit thereon. In *Duckwari plc v Offerventure and Another* [1994] New Property Cases 109, the Court of Appeal held that the section applied whether or not the transfer of the non-cash assets was pursuant to an informal or unenforceable contract.
- Directors, when dealing with their company, are not able to rely on the statutory protection generally afforded to third parties where the board has exceeded any limitation on their powers under the company's constitution when entering into the transaction, and any such contract will be voidable (s 322A; see above, 5.6).
- A company, without the approval of shareholders, is unable to enter into a service contract for more than five years with a director, which cannot be terminated by the company by a period of notice or which

can only be terminated in specified circumstances (s 319). Anti-avoidance provisions are included so that a director cannot enter into a further service contract which, when taken with his existing or immediately preceding service agreement, would extend, in aggregate, the period to over five years. Failure to comply with the terms of this section will result in the term being void and replaced by a provision entitling the company to terminate the agreement on reasonable notice.

- A company is not able to make payments to directors for compensation for loss of office or in connection with retirement from office unless the payment is disclosed to and approved by shareholders (s 312). This provision does not apply to '*bona fide* payments' by way of damages for breach of contract or by way of pension in respect of past services (s 316(3)).

- The Act contains detailed restrictions on the ability of a company or members of its group to provide loans to its directors. Broadly, in relation to private companies, the general rule is that such companies are prohibited from making a loan to their directors or those of its holding company or entering into any guarantee or providing any security in connection with such a loan (s 330). In addition, various indirect arrangements are covered so that the same result cannot be achieved by another person lending the money and then assigning the loan to the company or the company entering into back-to-back loan arrangements with another person who would then lend the money to the director. There are then a number of detailed exceptions to this general rule. In particular, the following are permitted:
  o loans not exceeding £5,000 (s 334);
  o loans of up to £20,000 provided to directors to meet expenditure incurred or to be incurred by him for the purpose of the company or for the purpose of enabling him properly to perform his duties as an officer of the company, but only if the approval of shareholders is obtained either prior to the grant of the loan or at the next AGM (s 337).

- A director who authorises or permits the company to enter into a transaction knowing or having reasonable cause to believe that it is in contravention of s 330 is guilty of an offence and the loan is able to be avoided at the instance of the company.

- Section 310 prohibits a company from providing its officers or auditors with an indemnity from liability that would otherwise attach to such persons in respect of any negligence, default, breach of duty

or breach of trust of which such persons may be guilty in relation to the company. This is subject to two important exceptions:
- a company is able to purchase and maintain indemnity insurance for such persons;
- a company may indemnify officers and auditors against liability incurred in defending civil or criminal proceedings in which judgment is given in his favour or he is acquitted or in connection with an application to the court for relief in certain circumstances.

8.8 Disclosure

A director is required, at the time of his appointment, to notify a company of any interest that he has in the shares or debentures of his company or any member of its group (s 324(1)). Further, he is required to keep the company informed of any dealings in the shares and/or debentures as specified in s 324(2). Schedule 13 to the Act gives a very wide meaning as to whether a director is 'interested' in shares and it is expressed as including any interest of any kind whatsoever in shares or debentures. For example, para 4 of Sched 13 provides that, in a company in which a director exercises or controls one-third or more of the votes, the director will be treated as interested in any shares held by that company. The company is required to keep this information in an appropriate register (s 325; see above, 3.5).

8.9 Single member companies

The Companies (Single Member Private Limited Companies) Regulations 1992 (SI 1992/1699) provide for special rules where a single member company enters into a contract with its sole member and:
- that member is also a director or shadow director of the company; and
- the contract is not in the ordinary course of business.

In such a case, the contract must either be in writing or its terms are set out in a written memorandum or are recorded in the minutes of the first meeting of the directors of the company following the making of the contract. Failure to do so may result in the relevant officers being liable to a fine but will not affect the validity of the contract.

8.10 Disqualification of directors

The court is able to disqualify a person from acting as a director on the grounds set out in the Company Directors Disqualification Act 1986. In summary, these grounds are as follows:

- Where a person has been convicted of an indictable offence in connection with the promotion, formation, management or liquidation of a company (s 2). This ground has been widely defined by the Courts. For example, in *R v Goodman* [1993] 2 All ER 789, it was held that a director who was found guilty of insider dealing was 'convicted of an indictable offence ... in connection with the ... management of a company', since the test was whether the offence had some relevant factual connection with the management of the company and not whether the offence related to the management of the company, such as keeping accounts.
- Where a person has been 'persistently in default' in relation to the provisions of the companies legislation in respect of returns, accounts or other documents to be sent to Companies House (s 3).
- Where a person has been convicted of fraudulent trading under s 458 or any fraud in relation to the company whether as officer, liquidator or receiver (s 4).
- Where a person has been summarily convicted on three occasions within the last five years for breach of the companies legislation referred to in s 3 above (s 5).

The maximum period of disqualification is five years in the case of ss 3 and 5 and 15 years in the case of ss 2 and 4 (unless the disqualification order is made by a court of summary jurisdiction, in which case the period is five years).

In addition, the court must disqualify a director where it is satisfied that he is or has been a director of a company that has at any time become insolvent and that his conduct as a director makes him unfit to be concerned with the management of a company (s 6).

The court, in order to determine whether a person is unfit to be concerned in the management of a company, is to have regard to the matters set out in the Schedule to the Act. These include such matters as whether the director has been guilty of any misfeasance or breach of fiduciary duty in relation to the company or been involved in any misappropriation or retention of the company's money.

In *Re Barings plc (No 5)*, the court clarified the criteria and standards to be applied in assessing whether a disqualification order on this ground was appropriate.

In applying the Act:
- the court should consider the director's conduct cumulatively and take into account any extenuating circumstances in assessing whether it had fallen below the standard required;
- the director's responsibility for the cause of the company becoming insolvent should be assessed broadly and not by reference to strict legal concepts of causation;
- where the allegation against the director is one of incompetence without dishonesty, this must be demonstrated to a very high degree;
- it is not necessary to demonstrate that the person in question is unfit to be involved in the management of any company in any role;
- a finding of breach of duty by the director is neither necessary nor sufficient for a finding of unfitness.

The Insolvency Bill, which is currently before Parliament, proposes changes to the current procedure for disqualification of directors. Where a director of an insolvent company agrees, a 'fast track' administrative disqualification could be initiated, avoiding the need for court proceedings. The Secretary of State for Trade and Industry would have the power to accept a 'disqualification undertaking' from such a director not to act as a director, liquidator, receiver or manager, or to take any part in the promotion, formation or management of a company. The undertaking would remain in force for a specified period of between two and 15 years and the restrictions could only be lifted with leave of the court. The aim of the legislation is to prevent delays in the processing of disqualification cases by the courts due to lack of judicial time.

9 Meetings

9.1 Types of meetings

There are three types of company meetings:

(a) general meetings of shareholders, which are required to be held to authorise or approve those matters specified in the articles or the Act. A general meeting may be either an AGM, the first of which is required to be held within 18 months of a company's incorporation and thereafter at intervals of not more than 15 months (s 366); or an extraordinary general meeting, being any general meeting other than an AGM;

(b) meetings of a particular class of shareholders (see above, 7.6);

(c) board meetings at which the directors meet for the purpose of making decisions relating to the management of the company.

9.2 Convening general meetings

A general meeting of the company will usually be convened by a resolution of the board of directors. In addition, the directors must convene a meeting when:

- requisitioned to do so by members holding at least one-10th of the paid up voting share capital of the company (s 368); or
- an auditor's notice of resignation is accompanied by: (a) a statement of circumstances which he considers should be brought to the company's attention; and (b) a signed requisition (s 392A).

The directors have to convene a meeting within 21 days of the requisition and the meeting must be held within 28 days of the giving of the notice (ss 368(4), (8) and 392A(5)) (notwithstanding that Table A refers to the meeting being held eight weeks from the date of requisition (reg 37)). If the directors do not convene a meeting within 21 days, the members (but not the auditors) are able to do so. Accordingly, unless the meeting can be held on short notice, the directors will, where an ordinary resolution is to be passed, need to convene the meeting at the latest 11 days after the receipt of the requisition (on the assumption that the company has Table A articles) or, in the case of a special resolution, four days after receipt (see below, 9.3).

If the articles are silent, two or more members holding not less than one-10th of the issued share capital may call a meeting (s 370).

If a company has Table A articles, then, if there are not sufficient directors in the UK to have a board meeting in order to convene a general meeting, a meeting is able to be convened by a single director or any member (reg 37).

The court has a residual power to convene meetings where it would otherwise be impracticable so to do (s 371).

9.3 Notices of general meeting

9.3.1 Length of notice

Subject to the points mentioned below, at least 21 days' notice must be given of all AGMs and extraordinary general meetings at which special resolutions are to be passed. In all other cases (that is, extraordinary general meetings where ordinary or extraordinary resolutions are to be passed), general meetings of a limited company must be held on at least 14 days' notice. Any provision in articles which attempts to shorten this period is void (s 369).

Table A requires 21 clear days' notice (that is, excluding the date on which the notice is despatched and the date of the meeting) to be given of AGMs and meetings at which special resolutions or resolutions appointing directors are to be proposed. The requirement to hold other meetings is 14 clear days' notice (reg 38). The English (but not Scottish) courts have held that, in any event, notwithstanding the provisions of the articles, special resolutions must be held on 21 clear days' notice (*Re Hector Whaling Ltd* [1936] Ch 208). In addition, it is also necessary to review the provisions contained in the articles regarding service of notices. Table A provides that a notice is deemed received 48 hours after posting (reg 115), although it is probably not possible to rely on this presumption if the company knows that shareholders will not have received notice by such time, for example, in a postal strike (*Bradman v Trinity Estates plc* (1989) 5 BCC 33). Accordingly, in calculating the number of days for calling a meeting, it is necessary to exclude the day on which the notice is posted and the two following days (where the reference is to clear days), so that the meeting at which a special resolution is proposed can be held on the 25th day from the date on which the notice was posted.

General meetings can be held on shorter notice than referred to above, provided that:
- in the case of AGMs, all the members agree to the proposed date (s 369(3));
- in all other cases, a majority in number of all shareholders representing at least 95% in nominal capital of the shares giving a right to attend and vote at the meeting agree to the date (ss 369(4) and 378(3)). This percentage may be reduced to 90% if an appropriate elective resolution has been passed (see below, 10.3.4).

The articles can provide for longer periods than those referred to above, which are the statutory minimum.

9.3.2 Persons entitled to receive notices

The Act provides that, unless the articles provide otherwise, notice of a meeting is to be served on every member in the manner in which notices are required to be served by Table A (s 370(2)). Regulation 38 of Table A requires that notices are served on:
- all members;
- all persons entitled to share in consequence of death or bankruptcy of a member;
- directors of the company;
- the auditors (auditors are entitled, in any event, to receive notices pursuant to the Act (s 390)).

However, in the case of joint holders, notice to the first named member on the register is sufficient notice to all holders; and no notice is required if the member's registered address is outside the UK and he has not given the company an address within the UK for the purpose of notices (reg 112).

At common law, failure to give notice to everyone who is entitled to receive it would invalidate the meeting. Table A avoids this problem by providing that the accidental omission to give notice to, or the non-receipt of notice by, any person will not affect the validity of the meeting (reg 39).

9.3.3 Contents of notices

The common law requires that members are informed of the time and place of the meeting and are given a sufficient indication of the business of the meeting in order for them to determine whether or not they need to attend. These requirements have broadly been incorporated in reg 38. In addition, the Act requires certain information to be expressly included in any notice:

- any special, extraordinary or elective resolution must be identified as such and the notice must set out the terms of the resolution verbatim and be accompanied by an adequate explanation of the proposals. In practice, although not strictly required, a similar approach is often taken for ordinary resolutions;
- if the meeting is an AGM, it must be described as such in the notice (s 366(1));
- the notice must include, with reasonable prominence, a statement that a member entitled to attend and vote at the meeting is entitled to appoint a proxy or, if it is permitted, proxies to attend and vote instead of him and that the proxy need not be a member (s 372(3)).

In respect of business to be conducted at AGMs, the articles may divide business between special and ordinary business. Where business is of an ordinary nature, it is not necessary for notice to be given of its content, since this will be apparent from the articles. Ordinary business will generally include the following matters: declaring a dividend; consideration of accounts, balance sheets and reports of the directors and auditors; the election of directors in place of those retiring; and the appointment of, and fixing the remuneration of, the auditors (see reg 52 of Table A, contained in the First Schedule to the Companies Act 1948). It should be noted that the existing Table A does not contain provision for any business at an AGM to constitute ordinary business and, if an appropriate amendment is not made, notice must be given of all matters to be considered at the relevant meeting.

9.4 Types of resolutions

9.4.1 Ordinary resolutions

An ordinary resolution is not defined in the Act but is a resolution passed at a general meeting held on at least 14 days' notice and agreed to by a majority of those present in person or by proxy at the meeting. An ordinary resolution is used whenever the Act or the articles of association do not require the passing of an elective, extraordinary or special resolution.

9.4.2 Special resolutions

A special resolution is a resolution passed at a general meeting held on at least 21 days' notice and agreed to by at least 75% of those members present in person or by proxy at the meeting. A special resolution is required to sanction certain matters required by the Act. For example, the following matters require special resolutions:

- changing the name of a company (s 28(1));
- alteration of the objects in the memorandum (s 4, see above, 5.9);
- disapplication of the pre-emption provisions contained in s 89 (s 95, see above, 7.3);
- reduction of company's capital (s 135, see above, 7.9);
- approval of the giving of financial assistance (s 155, see above, 7.5);
- authorisation of the off-market purchase of a company's own shares (s 164, see above, 7.8);
- approval of the purchase or redemption of a company's own shares out of capital (s 173, see above, 7.8);
- decision to wind up a company either voluntarily or by the court (ss 84(1)(b) and 122(a) of the Insolvency Act 1986).

9.4.3 Extraordinary resolutions

An extraordinary resolution is a resolution passed at a general meeting held on at least 14 days' notice and agreed to by at least 75% of those members present in person or by proxy at the meeting. An extraordinary resolution is required by the Insolvency Act 1986 to be used in circumstances relating to the winding-up of a company. In addition, variation of the rights of a class of shares often requires an extraordinary resolution to be passed at a separate meeting of that class (see above, 7.6).

9.4.4 Elective resolutions

An elective resolution is a resolution passed at a general meeting of shareholders held on at least 21 days' notice (unless all the members entitled to attend and vote at the meeting agree to short notice s 379A(2A)) and agreed to by all shareholders entitled to attend and vote at the meeting in order to dispense with certain administrative provisions of the Act (s 379A; see below, Chapter 10).

9.4.5 Written resolutions

(a) The common law

The common law has recognised the effectiveness of written resolutions for many years: see, for example, *Cane v Jones* [1980] 1 WLR 1451. Written resolutions obviate the need for meetings by getting all the shareholders to agree to a particular resolution. Regulation 53 of Table A provides for written resolutions:

> A resolution in writing executed by or on behalf of each member who would have been entitled to vote upon it if it had been proposed at a general meeting at which he was present shall be as effectual as if it had been passed at a general meeting duly convened and held and may consist of several instruments in the like form each executed by or on behalf of one or more members.

There are, however, a number of problems associated with using written resolutions at common law or under the articles:

- There is some doubt as to whether a written resolution can effectively pass a special or extraordinary resolution.
- A written resolution cannot be used where the Act specifically refers to an act being done or approval given by the company in general meeting or by ordinary resolution in order to effect a reduction of capital. For example, s 121 permits a company to increase its share capital but the section provides that this power may only be exercised in general meeting.
- It is not possible to use a written resolution where the business of the meeting includes receipt of accounts or any other matter concerning the auditors or where the meeting is requisitioned by the members.

In those cases specified above, it will be necessary to use the statutory procedure (see below); in other cases, it will be administratively easier to use the procedure under the articles since it will not be necessary to involve the auditors. In fact, following the coming into force of the Deregulation (Resolutions of Private Companies) Order 1996 (SI 1996/1471), s 381C makes it clear that any rule of law or enactment (and Table A is embodied in a statutory instrument) providing for written resolutions is expressly preserved and that the procedure under s 381A does not prejudice any existing power under the articles.

(b) The statutory procedure

Section 113 of the Companies Act 1989 introduced a new s 381A to the Act which provides for written resolutions in lieu of a general or class meeting to be passed, without a period of notice, if signed by all the members of the company who at the date of the resolution would be entitled to attend and vote at such meetings. There are a number of general points to note on the section:

- every member has a right of veto;
- it can only be used by a private company;
- the signatures need not be on a single document provided each is on a document which accurately states the terms of the resolution. It should be noted that the documents distributed to the shareholders need not be identical and accordingly the resolution could be included in an individual letter to shareholders.

The date of the resolution is the date when the resolution is signed by or on behalf of the last member to sign. Only those members who could vote at a general meeting are required to sign the resolution. Accordingly, the signature of any one of joint shareholders will suffice. Likewise, where a shareholder dies and his shares are disenfranchised until the personal representatives are registered as members, the holding can be properly ignored until such time as the personal representatives are registered. If, however, the composition of shareholders changes whilst the resolution is doing the rounds, it will be necessary to get the new member to sign the resolution.

The procedure for the passing of written resolutions is subject to review by the company's auditors. Section 381B provides that a copy of any written resolution that is to be proposed under s 381A must be sent to the auditors, or they must be informed of the contents of the written resolution at or before the time that resolution is supplied to a member for signature.

The written resolution procedure cannot be used in two specified circumstances (as set out in Pt I of Sched 15A):

- an ordinary resolution under s 303 removing a director before the expiration of his period of office;
- an ordinary resolution under s 391 removing an auditor before the expiration of his term of office.

Sched 15A specifies that various additional documents have to be sent with the written resolution in specified instances in order for the resolution to be validly passed. The general rule is that, whenever documents are required to be despatched with the notice of meeting or displayed prior to a resolution being passed, a written resolution can be used provided that the document concerned is sent to shareholders at or before the time the resolution is sent to him for his signature. Details of the resolutions referred to in Pt II of Sched 15A are set out in Table II, below).

A record of the resolution (and of the signatures) is to be entered into the company's minute book. Such record, if purporting to be signed by a director or secretary, is evidence of the resolution and all the procedural requirements are deemed to have been complied with unless the contrary can be shown.

It will be necessary for such resolutions to be filed at Companies House, within 15 days of their being passed, if they are, in effect, passing an extraordinary or special resolution. Section 381A(6) expressly states that any reference in an enactment to a special, extraordinary or elective resolution is deemed to include a written resolution having the same effect. Furthermore, s 381A(5) provides that any reference in an enactment to a resolution being passed is deemed to be a reference to the date when all the members sign.

The procedure contained in the Act is broader than that under the common law or reg 53:

- It applies whether or not a company has reg 53 or a similar article in its articles of association.
- It puts beyond doubt that the written resolution can effect a special or extraordinary resolution as expressly stated in s 381A(6).
- Section 381A(4) states that the written resolution is to be treated as if it had been passed at a general meeting or a class meeting and any reference in any enactment to a meeting at which a resolution is passed or to members voting in favour of the resolution shall be construed accordingly. Therefore, a written resolution under s 381A can be used to pass a resolution where the Act would normally require a physical meeting to be held, such as pursuant to s 121, provided the requirements of Pt II of Sched 15A are complied with.

Table II

Resolution	Documents to be supplied with written resolution
Special resolution under s 95(2) disapplication of pre-emption rights to specific allotments of equity securities	Written statement from directors specifying information set out in s 95(5): • reasons for making recommendation • amount to be paid to the company in respect of the equity securities • directors' justification of that amount
Special resolution under s 155(4) or (5) permitting a private company to give financial assistance in certain circumstances	Documents specified in s 157(4)(a): directors' statutory declaration with auditors' report
Special resolution under s 164(2), (3) and (7) – authorising, varying or revoking authority for the company to make an off market purchase of its own shares or varying an existing contract so approved	Documents referred to in s 164(6) and s 164(7): • a copy of the purchase agreement • a copy of variation to the terms of the contract (A member holding shares to which the resolution relates need not sign)
Special resolution under s 173(2) approving redemption or purchase of own shares out of capital	Documents specified in s 174(4): • directors' statutory declaration and auditors' report (A member holding shares to which the resolution relates need not sign)
Ordinary resolution under s 319 approving director's service contract of more than five years	The service contract itself – s 319(5)
Ordinary resolution under s 337 providing a director with funds to meet expenditure incurred for the purposes of the company or for him to properly perform his duties	Matters to be disclosed pursuant to s 337(4): • purpose of the expenditure incurred • the amount of funds to be provided by the company • the extent of the company's liability under any transaction which is or is connected with the thing in question

9.5 Representation at meetings

9.5.1 Proxies

A shareholder who is unable to attend a meeting is able to appoint another person (whether or not a shareholder) as his proxy to attend and speak at the meeting and vote on his behalf (s 372). This right must be prominently stated in any notice of meeting sent to members.

Unless the articles otherwise provide, a shareholder is not able to appoint more than one proxy to attend on the same occasion and proxies are not able to vote on a show of hands but only on a poll (see below, 9.6.3).

In order to be valid, the form of proxy must be delivered at the time and place stated by the articles. Table A provides that, for a proxy to be valid, it must be deposited at the registered office of the company or such other place specified in the notice at least 48 hours prior to the meeting (reg 62). Any provision in articles that requires proxies to be deposited more than 48 hours before the meeting is void (s 372(5)). A form of proxy may give the proxy total freedom as to how he is to vote or, alternatively, may give him voting instructions. Both types of appointment of a proxy are contained in regs 60 and 61.

9.5.2 Corporate representatives

Where a company is a member of a company, the Act provides that it may, by resolution of its directors or other governing body, appoint a representative for the purpose of general meetings (s 375). A corporate representative, unlike a proxy, is treated for all purposes as if he were a member and, accordingly, whilst a representative should bring evidence of his appointment to any meeting of the company, he is not required to deposit the form of appointment with the company prior to any meeting. In addition, a corporate representative is able to vote on a show of hands.

9.6 Proceedings at general meetings

9.6.1 Quorum

In order for a meeting to be constitutionally valid, it is necessary for a quorum to be present, although whether it has to be present throughout the meeting will depend on the articles. The Act provides that, unless the articles otherwise provide, two members personally present are a quorum (that is, proxies are not taken into account) (s 370(4)). Table A provides that two members present in person or by proxy, who are entitled to vote, will constitute a quorum and that the quorum must be present throughout the meeting (reg 40). However, s 370A provides that, notwithstanding any provision of the articles of a private company where a company has only one member, one member present in person or by proxy shall be a quorum. If a quorum is not present within half an hour, the meeting is to be adjourned until the same day next week at the same time and place or such other time and place as the directors shall determine (reg 41). It is usual to provide for a larger quorum in respect of class meetings; often, reference is made to members holding a stated percentage of the issued shares of the relevant class. In the absence of any provision in the articles, a quorum at class meetings is two persons present in person or by proxy, holding at least one-third in nominal value of issued shares of the relevant class, and at an adjourned meeting one person or proxy holding shares of the relevant class (s 125(6)).

9.6.2 Chairman

Unless the articles otherwise provide, any member elected by the members present at a meeting may be chairman of it (s 370(5)). Table A provides that the chairman of the board of directors or, in his absence, some other nominated director shall be chairman of the meeting. If such person is not present within 15 minutes of the specified time for the meeting, then one of the directors shall be chairman or, if no directors are present, the members are entitled to choose the chairman from those present (regs 42 and 43).

The chairman's function is to ensure that the business of the meeting is conducted in a proper and efficient manner, in accordance with the provisions of the Act and the articles. In addition, the chairman is given certain powers at common law which may be supplemented by the articles. For example, at common law, a chairman is able to adjourn the meeting in order to preserve order or where it is not possible for all the members present to effectively take part in the meeting (*Byng v London Life Association Ltd* (1989) 5 BCC 227). Table A enables the chairman to:

- adjourn the meeting with the consent of shareholders (reg 45);
- direct that a poll be taken and fix the manner in which it is taken and the time and place at which the results are announced (not more than 30 days after the date of the meeting) (regs 46, 49 and 51);

- have a casting vote (in addition to any other votes which he is entitled to cast) where there is an equality of votes either on a show of hands or a poll (reg 50);
- unless a poll is demanded, declare the results of the voting on a show of hands and any such declaration by the chairman is conclusive (reg 47).

9.6.3 Voting

Articles invariably provide for voting on any particular resolution to take place initially by a show of hands. Table A provides that every member, on a show of hands, has one vote, irrespective of the number of shares held by him (reg 54). Unless the articles otherwise provide, which Table A does not, a proxy is not able to vote on a show of hands (s 372(2)(c)).

After a show of hands has been conducted, if the result is not unanimous, it will usually be necessary to conduct a poll where the number of votes that can be cast by members will be related to the number of shares held by them. There are no restrictions upon proxies voting on a poll. Table A provides for one vote for each share held by a member (reg 54) but, obviously, this will depend on the class of shares held and the voting rights attached to them. Table A permits any of the following to demand a poll:

- the chairman;
- any two members who have the right to vote;
- members representing at least one-10th of total voting rights;
- members holding voting shares on which have been paid up, in aggregate, one-10th of the total amount paid up on all such shares (reg 46).

A proxy is permitted to join in or make a demand for a poll to the same extent as the member he represents (s 373(2)). A provision in the articles is void if an attempt is made to exclude the rights to demand a poll on any matter other than the appointment of a chairman or adjournment of a meeting. Further, a provision is void if a poll is required to be demanded by five or more members having voting rights or members having more than 10% of the voting rights or paid up share capital (s 373(1)).

9.7 Amendments to resolutions

Once a notice has been sent to members, the extent to which amendments can be made at the general meeting at which it is to be considered will depend on the nature of the resolution:

- Special and extraordinary resolutions can only be amended to the extent that such amendments do not affect the substance of the resolution, for example, grammatical or typographical corrections. This is a strict rule and there is no room for a *de minimis* exception (*Re Moorgate Mercantile Holdings Ltd* [1980] 1 All ER 40).
- Ordinary resolutions may be amended provided that the amendment is reasonably within the scope of the business to be conducted at the meeting and does not impose further obligations upon the company.

9.8 Board meetings

The procedure for board meetings should be set out in the articles. Table A contains the following provisions:

- it is not necessary to give directors absent from the UK notice of any meeting (reg 88);
- the quorum is to be fixed by the directors and until fixed is to be two directors (reg 89);
- resolutions of the board are to be decided by a majority of votes and the chairman has a casting vote in the case of a tie on any issue (reg 88);
- directors are able to pass resolutions by written resolution signed by all the directors (reg 93).

In all other respects, the directors are able to regulate their own proceedings. Accordingly, for example, Table A does not specify the amount of notice for a board meeting to be called and the directors are free to determine the appropriate amount of notice. The directors are able to delegate some or all of their powers to a committee if the articles so permit. Regulation 72 authorises the directors to delegate their powers to a committee consisting of one or more directors. There are a number of points to note in respect of delegation of authority:

- The directors, in delegating their powers to a committee, are not able to abdicate responsibility for those matters so delegated and are required to monitor effectively and supervise the committee's performance. See the discussion of *Re Westmid Packing Services Ltd* [1998] 2 All ER 124 above, 8.6.

- If it is intended that the committee is to delegate its powers to a director or another committee, the power of sub-delegation must be expressly contained in the resolution of the board establishing the committee.
- In the light of *Guinness v Saunders* [1988] BCLC 43, the courts are taking a more critical view of the delegation of powers and, accordingly, it is important to ensure that there is express authority in the articles for the particular power to be delegated.

10 The Elective Regime

10.1 Introduction

The Companies Act 1989 introduced the concept of an elective resolution, which allows a company to dispense with certain requirements of the Act. Lord Strathclyde, who introduced this measure in the House of Lords, said that it was intended both to create 'a valuable element of flexibility into the management of small companies' and to 'bring the law into line with commercial reality' (that is, many small companies already ignore a number of Companies Act provisions).

10.2 The elective resolution

At least 21 days' notice is required of a meeting at which an elective resolution is proposed (unless all the members of the company entitled to attend and vote at the meeting agreed to short notice (s379A(2A))) and the resolution itself must be agreed to by all the members of the company entitled to attend and vote at the meeting (s 379A).

There are a number of points to note about elective resolutions:

- Any member can veto such a resolution and, accordingly, it will only be appropriate for shareholder/management companies or wholly-owned subsidiaries of private or public companies.
- It can be passed by means of a unanimous written resolution passed in accordance with the provisions of ss 381A–382A (see above, 9.4.5).
- It can only be used for private companies and, accordingly, ceases to have effect if the company is re-registered as a public company.
- It can be revoked by an ordinary resolution.
- It can be passed or revoked notwithstanding any provision in the company's memorandum or articles of association.

- The resolution (or a resolution revoking an elective resolution) is required to be filed at Companies House within 15 days of its being passed.

10.3 Requirements that can be dispensed with

10.3.1 Section 80 of the Companies Act 1985

Section 80 requires that the directors of a company have the consent of members prior to the issue of any shares. The authority must state the maximum number of securities over which it is given, and the maximum length of any such authority is five years (see above, 7.2). An elective resolution passed pursuant to s 80A will enable the authority to be given for any fixed period exceeding five years or for an indefinite period of time. The authority may be revoked or varied in general meeting and a fixed period can be renewed. If an election is subsequently revoked and the s 80 authority was given for an indefinite period or for more than five years, then the authority will expire forthwith if the authority was given more than five years ago; otherwise, the authority will continue to have effect until the expiry of five years (s 80A(7)). Section 80 authority can only be given in relation to existing share capital and, therefore, even if the directors have authority to issue shares pursuant to s 80 for an indefinite period of time, any subsequent increase in share capital will necessitate a new authority to be obtained.

10.3.2 Annual general meetings

The general rule under s 366 is that an AGM must be held in each year; the first AGM must be held within the first 18 months of incorporation and not more than 15 months must elapse between the date of one AGM and another. A private company may elect to dispense with the holding of AGMs required by s 366, and this is intended to complement the provisions concerning written resolutions so that shareholders need never physically meet during the year.

The election has effect for the year in which it is given and for subsequent years. Accordingly, it must be given within the first 18 months of incorporation if it is intended to dispense with the first AGM. An elective resolution does not affect any liability already incurred for non-compliance with the requirements of the Act in previous years (s 366A).

This provision is not, however, as radical as it first appears: merely because a company dispenses with the AGM does not mean that it can dispense with all the business to be conducted at the AGM; other elective resolutions will be required to effect this. Furthermore, it is possible for any single shareholder to require the holding of an AGM (without revoking the elective resolution which would require an ordinary resolution) by giving notice to the company not later than three months prior to the end of the year in which the AGM would otherwise be required to be held. This is obviously desirable protection for minority shareholders, since otherwise once their consent had originally been obtained for the passing of the elective resolution, the directors could be forever safeguarded from being challenged on the management of the company.

The section contemplates only a general power dispensing with AGMs and does not seem to provide for a specific resolution, for example, not requiring AGMs for the first five years. Accordingly, it would be necessary to revoke the elective resolution after the time that it was no longer intended to apply. If an election ceases to have effect, the company is not required to hold an AGM in that year if the revocation takes effect less than three months before the end of the year in which the AGM would otherwise require to be held.

10.3.3 Laying of accounts and reports

The general rule is that the directors of a company are required to lay copies of the company's annual accounts, the directors' report and the auditors' report on the accounts before the general meeting (s 241). The period allowed for laying and delivering reports and accounts for a private company is 10 months after the end of the relevant accounting reference period (s 244).

A private company may elect to dispense with the laying of accounts and reports before the company in general meeting (s 252). Clearly, this goes hand in hand with the election to dispense with the AGM and, usually, both elections will be made at the same time. If this election has not been made and the requirement to dispense with an AGM has been made, then it will be necessary to convene a general meeting for the purpose of laying accounts, so reducing the effectiveness of dispensing with AGMs.

Once the election becomes effective, the requirement to lay accounts before the AGM is complied with by sending to shareholders these accounts, together with, in cases of qualified accounts (that is, where the auditors cannot say, without qualification, that the accounts give a true and fair view of the state of affairs of the company), a statement explaining the qualification not less than 28 days before the end of the period allowed for laying accounts. In addition to the accounts, a statement must be included setting out the member's right to require a meeting. The election has effect in relation to the accounts in respect of the financial year in which the election is made and subsequent financial years. Revocation, likewise, applies to the accounts in the financial year that the revocation is made.

Within the 28 day period from the date on which accounts were sent out, any member or auditor may, by notice in writing to the company at its registered office, require a meeting to be held for the purpose of laying the accounts and reports (s 253(2)). If the directors do not convene a meeting within 21 days from the date of the notice, the member or auditor can convene the meeting himself within a three month period. It is expressly provided that the directors have not duly convened a meeting if they convene a meeting for a date more than 28 days after the date of the notice convening it. Any reasonable expenses of the member convening the appropriate meeting in default of the directors are to be paid by the company and reclaimed from the directors. It should be noted that an election to dispense with the laying of reports and accounts or with the holding of an AGM must be stated in the annual return.

10.3.4 Short notice provisions

Sections 369(4) and 378(3) enable a general meeting (other than an AGM), whether or not a special or extraordinary resolution is proposed, to be held on short notice, provided that members holding at least 95% of the nominal share value so agree. The 1989 Act enables shareholders to elect that this figure can be reduced to an amount of not less than 90%. The exact percentage can be left undefined to be determined by the general meeting at a later date.

10.3.5 Dispensation with appointment of auditors

A private company may elect to dispense with the obligation to appoint auditors annually. This, again, will go hand in hand with the election not to hold an AGM and to dispense with the laying of accounts at a general meeting. The general rule is that auditors are to be appointed at: (a) the general meeting at which accounts are laid (s 385); or (b) if an election dispensing with the laying of accounts has been made, at a general meeting convened within a 28 day period of the accounts being despatched to members (s 385A). When the election to dispense with appointing auditors is in force, the auditors are deemed to be re-appointed for each succeeding financial year on the expiry of the time for appointing auditors. The usual safeguard has been included – a member may, by notice in writing to the company, propose that the appointment of auditors be terminated and the directors are required to convene a meeting, within 14 days, for a date not more than 28 days after the date that the notice was given in order to consider the appropriate resolution. If the directors do not convene a meeting within 14 days, the member may do so himself within three months of that date. If a resolution is so passed, then the auditors will not be re-appointed when next they would be and, if a notice is deposited within 14 days of the accounts being sent out to members, then any deemed re-appointment shall not have effect for that financial year. A member can only exercise this right once in a financial year. If the election is revoked, the auditors continue in office until the general meeting at which the accounts are laid or until another appointment under s 385A.

10.3.6 The future

Section 117 of the Companies Act 1989 permits the Secretary of State, by regulations, to make provisions enabling private companies to elect to dispense with compliance to Companies Act requirements, provided that these relate 'primarily' to the internal administration and procedure of companies. No regulations have, at present, been made under this section.

11 Execution of Documents by a Company

11.1 Introduction

Contracts may be executed by a company under hand or under seal. It will be necessary to execute documents under seal where:
- there is no consideration passing from the company under the relevant contract;
- statute or the articles require a particular document to be under seal;
- it is intended to increase the limitation period. Actions under a sealed document can be brought 12 years from the date of the contract, whereas it is only six years in the case of contracts under hand.

11.2 Documents under hand

In respect of documents that do not have to be under seal, the procedure for execution is relatively simple. On the assumption that the board meeting approves the document, it will give named director(s) power to sign the agreement on behalf of the company. A suggested form of resolution is as follows:

> IT IS RESOLVED THAT the agreement between X Limited and the Company relating to the purchase by the Company of the business known as 'Danny's Shoes' be hereby approved and that any director be authorised to sign the same on behalf of the Company with power to make such amendments to the agreement [other than in relation to price] as he may, in his absolute discretion, think fit.

Where a person is signing on behalf of a company, the appropriate attestation clause on a document would be:

Signed by [ ] for and on behalf of [Limited].

In relation to a third party contracting with the company, it would be advisable for him, because of the problems with s 35 and 35A (see above, Chapter 5) to review the authority of the person purporting to execute the document on behalf of the company. This will be particularly the case where a non-director is executing documents on behalf of the company, since that person may not have ostensible authority to bind the company.

11.3 Documents under seal

A company may seal a document in one of two ways. It can either affix the company seal in the presence of appropriate witnesses or use the procedure set out in s 36A.

11.3.1 Execution by affixing the company seal

A company seal is a device that impresses the name of the company onto a document. The provisions contained in the articles have to be followed before it can be affixed to any document. Table A provides that the seal is only able to be used under the authority of directors or an appropriately authorised committee. Further, the directors may determine who shall sign any instrument to which the seal is to be affixed and until so determined it shall be signed by a director and the secretary or a second director (reg 101). Despite the introduction of s 36A (see below, 11.3.2), it may still be advantageous for a company to retain a seal, since the seal can be official in the presence of any person authorised by the directors and not, as in s 35A, only in the presence of two directors or a director and the secretary.

The appropriate board resolution for a document to be executed under seal would be:

IT IS RESOLVED that the Company seal be attached to [ ] in the presence of any two directors or a director and the secretary.

Where the company seal is being affixed to a document, the appropriate attestation clause on the document should be:

The Company Seal of [Limited] was hereunto affixed in the presence of:
Director
Director/Secretary

In relation to third parties, if the seal is affixed in the presence of a director and secretary (but not two directors), then the third party will be able to rely on the presumption of due execution contained in s 74 of the Law of Property Act 1925. Accordingly, where the seal is affixed otherwise and because of the concerns over the protection afforded by s 35A (see above, Chapter 5), it will be necessary for a third party to review the appropriate articles to ensure that the formalities have been complied with.

11.3.2 Execution pursuant to s 36A

As a result of the change made to the 1985 Act by the Companies Act 1989, a company is able, should it so wish, to dispense with the need for a company seal by using the procedure set out in s 36A.

Section 36A(4) provides that a document signed by a director and the secretary or two directors and expressed (in whatever form of words) to be executed by the company has the same effect as if executed under the common seal.

Using this method of execution will give rise to a rebuttable presumption that, provided that the document makes it clear on its face that it is intended to take effect as a deed, it will take effect on execution (s 36A(5)).

In addition, there is an irrebuttable presumption in favour of a purchaser that a document is duly executed by the company if it purports to be signed by a director and a secretary or two directors. Furthermore, where it makes it clear on its face that it is intended by the persons making it to be a deed, there is an irrebuttable presumption that it is delivered upon being executed (s 36A(6)). A 'purchaser' is defined as a 'purchaser in good faith for valuable consideration and includes a lessee, mortgagee or other person who for valuable consideration acquires an interest in property'. Accordingly, if it is not intended for the document to be immediately delivered upon execution and the document leaves the control of the company, such as in some form of escrow arrangement, the use of the company seal may, in some circumstances, be preferred.

The appropriate board resolution for a document being executed under s 36A would be:

> IT IS RESOLVED THAT [   ] be executed as a deed and signed by any two directors or any director and the secretary.

The form of attestation where a company is executing a document in accordance with s 36A is:

Signed as a deed by [name of company] [signature]

acting by [name of director] a director [signature]

and [name of director or secretary]

[a director or secretary]

11.3.3 Execution by a foreign company

In relation to companies incorporated outside Great Britain, the Foreign Companies (Execution of Documents) Regulations 1994 (SI 1994/950, as amended (see above, 1.1)) apply. The Regulations provide that a foreign company can execute a deed:

- by affixing its common seal (if it has one);
- in any manner permitted by the laws of the territory in which the company was incorporated for the execution of documents by such a company;
- if the document is expressed to be executed by the company and is signed by person(s) who, in accordance with the laws of the territory where the company is incorporated, are acting under the authority of that company.

Again, the irrebuttable presumption in s 36A(6) of delivery or execution (see above, 11.3.2) will arise where the signatory of the document is acting under the authority of that company and it is clear upon the document's face that it is intended by the person making it to be a deed.

12 Minority Shareholder Rights

12.1 The rule in *Foss v Harbottle*

The rule in *Foss v Harbottle* (1843) 2 Hare 461 provides, in essence, that, if a wrong is done to a company, then it is the company who is the proper party to bring an action. The rule is designed to avoid shareholders bringing a multiplicity of actions. However, its application may lead to injustice where the company is controlled by the wrongdoers, since it would be they who would determine whether proceedings ought to be brought. Accordingly, a number of exceptions have been established to the rule where a minority shareholder is able to bring an action on behalf of the company:

- where the act is beyond the objects of the company or is illegal;
- where the matter is one which could only be validly done by a special majority of members (in other words, the matter cannot be ratified by means of an ordinary resolution);
- where the member has a personal right, for example, a claim based on enforcement of the articles pursuant to s 14 (see above, Chapter 6). In this case, the action would be brought by the shareholder in his personal capacity and not on behalf of the company. The shareholder must be able to demonstrate direct personal loss and not merely a general loss to the company which all shareholders suffer;
- where the act amounts to a fraud on the minority. In order to use this exception, the shareholder must be able to demonstrate:
  - some form of equitable fraud, such as expropriation of the company's property or even negligence by a director, will suffice, but only where he profits from such negligence (*Daniels v Daniels* [1978] Ch 406);
  - that the wrongdoers are in control of the company – it is not entirely clear what constitutes control but the Court of Appeal

in *Prudential Assurance Co Ltd v Newman Industries Ltd* (No 2) [1982] Ch 204 appeared to accept that control meant *de facto* control and not just control through holding a majority of the shares; and

○ that a majority of independent shareholders support the action on behalf of the company (*Smith v Croft (No 2)* [1988] Ch 114).

In practice, this exception is of very limited use for minority shareholders, since the amount of time and expense required in order to establish their *locus standi* to bring an action on behalf of the company is often disproportionate to the remedy actually achieved. In any event, any damages awarded go to the company rather than the individual shareholder, since the action is brought by the shareholder on behalf of the company.

12.2 Section 459

Section 459 provides that a shareholder is able to seek relief from the court on the basis that:

> ... the company's affairs are being or have been conducted in a manner which is unfairly prejudicial to the interests of its members generally or of some part of its members (including at least himself) or that any actual or proposed act or omission of the company (including an act or omission on its behalf) is or would be so prejudicial.

The test of whether unfair prejudice has occurred is objective. The question is whether a reasonable bystander observing the consequences of the conduct complained of would regard it as having unfairly prejudiced the petitioner's interests (*Re RA Noble & Sons (Clothing) Ltd* [1983] BCLC 273). Accordingly, there is no requirement for the petitioner to establish that the defendant was acting in bad faith or that he intended to cause unfair prejudice to the petitioner.

The conduct of the petitioner may be a relevant factor for the court to take into account in determining whether a claim is successful under this section or, indeed, the nature of any remedy granted. Although there is no express requirement in the section for the petitioner to come to the court with clean hands, it has been held that the petitioner's conduct will be taken into account in determining whether or not the conduct was unfair. For example, in *Re RA Noble & Sons (Clothing) Ltd* it was held that, whilst the petitioner was prejudiced, in that he was excluded from the management of the company, it was not unfair because he had lost interest in the business and accordingly had brought it upon himself.

It seems clear that mismanagement, in itself, is not sufficient to found a claim under s 459, although if the negligence amounted to a breach of a director's duty of skill and care it may be. It will undoubtedly do so where the negligence benefits the majority shareholder in some way, for example, where an asset is sold to a majority shareholder at an undervalue (*Re Elgindata Ltd* [1991] BCLC 959).

There is some doubt over whether the petitioner has to suffer the prejudice in his capacity as shareholder or whether relief can be sought under the section if the prejudice is suffered by him as, for example, a director (see *Re A Company No 004475 of 1982* [1983] 2 WLR 381; *Re A Company No 002567 of 1982* [1983] 2 All ER 854). In *O'Neill v Phillips* [1999] 1 WLR 1092, the House of Lords stated that the requirement that prejudice must be suffered as a member 'should not be too narrowly or technically construed'. It appears from the judicial *dicta* in a number of cases that the courts will treat shareholders in a small private company as having a legitimate expectation as to involvement in the management of the business, which will be protected by the section. For example, in *R & H Electric and Another v Haden Bill Electrical Ltd* [1995] 2 BCLC 280, the court found that a shareholder, who had provided a loan through a company that he controlled, had a legitimate expectation that he would continue to be involved in the management of the business for so long as his company remained a significant loan creditor. Accordingly, relief was granted when that shareholder was removed from the board prior to the repayment of the loan.

The House of Lords in *O'Neill v Phillips* has, however, held that the failure to meet a shareholder's 'legitimate expectation' would not generally amount to unfair prejudice in the absence of some more precise agreement between the parties.

The judgment clarified and restricted the circumstances in which a s 459 petition would be granted as follows:

- 'unfair prejudice' would generally require a breach of the terms upon which the shareholder had agreed the company's affairs would be conducted; however
- as the relationship between a company and its shareholders would be considered by equity to be a contract of good faith, unfairness would also arise where a legal right (such as a power under the Companies Act) was used in a manner equity would regard as contrary to good faith.

An example of a situation where this second limb would come into play would be where the company's exercise of its legal rights would conflict with (not necessarily contractually enforceable) promises the parties had exchanged.

The court proposed that a useful test for unfair prejudice under this second limb would be:

> Whether the exercise of the power in question would be contrary to what the parties, by words or conduct, have actually agreed.

On the facts of *O'Neill v Phillips*, whilst Mr O'Neill, a shareholder and director of the company in question, could have been said to have a 'legitimate expectation' to be allotted additional shares and to continue profit sharing, there had been no promise or agreement to this effect and hence his petition failed.

Since the section's amendment by the Companies Act 1989, a claim will be able to be brought under it even where the prejudice affects all members equally. Accordingly, it is now possible to bring an action under this section where the directors, through an improper motive, refuse to pay a dividend to the membership. However, in order to bring such a claim, it is necessary to show that there existed some agreement or promise as to the payment of a dividend as evidenced by some commercial agreement. It is not sufficient merely to claim that the company has not generally been managed in the way contemplated by the petitioner (*Re Saul D Harrison & Sons plc* [1994] BCC 475).

Once unfair prejudice is established, the court has complete discretion as to remedy granted. In particular, it can make an order regulating the conduct of the company, injunct the company from acting in a particular manner, authorise civil proceedings to be brought by or on behalf of the company or require the shares of any member of the company to be purchased (s 461).

Whilst s 459 has traditionally been considered a remedy for minority shareholders, the court in *Morris and Others v Hateley and Another* [1999] 2 BCLC 171 noted that the wording of s 459 does not preclude an action by a majority shareholder, for example, where the shareholder's voting rights do not accord with its shareholding. However, as a majority shareholder will generally have the power to pass any resolution to bring to an end a prejudicial state of affairs, the circumstances in which such a petition could succeed would be limited.

12.3 Just and equitable winding-up

Section 122(1)(g) of the Insolvency Act 1986 permits a court to wind up a company on the ground that it is just and equitable so to do. There are a number of points to note about this remedy:

- In order for a member to seek a winding-up order, he must be a contributory, that is, a person liable to contribute to the assets of a company on winding-up (s 79 of the Insolvency Act 1986); for example, a member who holds partly-paid shares. The courts permit the holders of fully paid up shares to present a petition provided that they establish a tangible interest in the company's winding-up and, therefore, no application can be made by them if the company is insolvent.
- The member must have held his shares for at least six months during the 18 months prior to the commencement of the winding-up or the shares must have devolved on him through the death of a former member (s 124(2) of the Insolvency Act 1986).
- The court will not make an order if some other remedy is available to the petitioner and he is acting unreasonably in seeking to have the company wound up instead of pursuing that other remedy.
- The court will apply general equitable principles in determining whether to make an order under this section and, accordingly, the petitioner must come to the court with clean hands.

The circumstances in which the remedy can be used were outlined in *Ebrahami v Westbourne Galleries Ltd* [1973] AC 360. Lord Wilberforce, in this classic case, emphasised that the courts would:

> ... subject the exercise of legal rights to equitable considerations; that is of a personal character arising between one individual and another, which may make it unjust, or inequitable, to insist on legal rights, or to exercise them in a particular way.

In that case, a shareholder was removed as a director in accordance with (what is now) s 303 and the court held that the use of this legal right was inequitable in all the circumstances and the company should be dissolved. The House of Lords gave an indication as to the type of company in respect of which legal rights are subject to equitable considerations. These companies would have one or more of the following characteristics:

- A company formed or continued on the basis of a personal relationship involving mutual confidence, usually where a partnership is converted into a limited company.

- An agreement or understanding that some or all of the shareholders shall participate in the conduct of the business.
- Where there is a restriction upon the transfer of the members' interest in the company so that if confidence is lost, or one member is removed from management, he cannot take his stake and go elsewhere.

13 Charges and Debentures

13.1 The power to borrow

Almost all companies have an express power to borrow in their articles and, even if they do not, a power to borrow will be implied (*General Auction Estate and Monetary Co v Smith* [1891] 3 Ch 432). Furthermore, a company that has power to borrow also has implied power to charge its assets but not to give guarantees or secure the obligations of third parties (including its subsidiaries). Articles may contain restrictions on this power to borrow by limiting the amount of borrowing to, for example, a specified multiple of share capital and reserves. Table A does not contain any restriction on directors' power to borrow.

13.2 Types of debentures

A debenture is a written acknowledgment of a company's debt. It may be either unsecured or secured over the company's assets by means of a fixed or floating charge. It is important to ascertain whether a creditor has a fixed or a floating charge, since on a winding-up the priority of a creditor will depend on the nature of security held (see below, 13.4). It should be noted that the court, in determining the type of charge, will look to the substance of the security and not merely to the title accorded by the parties.

A fixed charge is a charge over defined assets, such as real property. A fixed charge can cover not only assets in existence but future assets, for example, a charge over book debts which may be paid to a company at some point in the future (*Siebe Gorman Ltd v Barclays Bank Ltd* [1979] 2 Lloyd's Rep 142). It is an essential feature of a fixed charge that the property subject to the charge cannot be dealt with until the consent of the chargee is obtained, and therefore it is inappropriate to take a fixed charge over a company's stock in trade since it would be impractical to obtain the chargee's consent each time it wished to sell its stock. In the *Siebe Gorman* case, all book debts of the company had to be paid into a bank account with the chargee bank and it was not free to deal with the debts in the ordinary course of its business. This case was distinguished in *Re Brightlife* [1987] Ch 200, where a fixed charge was purportedly taken over the future book debts of a company and, although the company covenanted not to deal with the debts, there was no requirement to pay the proceeds into its bank account. Accordingly, the court held that the charge amounted to a floating charge. The Court of Appeal in *Re New Bullas Trading* [1994] BCLC 485 held that, so long as the parties expressly agree, a valid fixed charge over uncollected book debts does not require that the chargee exercise control over the account into which the proceeds of realisation are paid. In that case, a debenture created a fixed charge over the book debts of the company and required the company to pay the monies into a designated account and to deal with such monies in accordance with any directions given by the debenture holder. In the absence of any such directions, the monies would be released from the fixed charge and become subject to a floating charge. The court held that the charge constituted a fixed charge.

A floating charge is a charge over the general undertaking of a company's property which allows the company to dispose freely of the assets (the subject of the charge) until an event of crystallisation occurs, usually, amongst other things, the appointment of a receiver or liquidator, when the charge becomes a fixed equitable charge. A floating charge has three main characteristics (*Re Yorkshire Woolcombers Association Ltd* [1903] 2 Ch 284, p 295):

(a) it is a charge on assets present and future;

(b) the class of assets is one which, in the ordinary course of business, would be changing from time to time;

(c) the charge contemplates that, until some future step is taken by the chargee, the company may continue its business in the ordinary way in relation to those assets.

The courts have expressly recognised, however, that even if all the requirements referred to above are not present, this does not necessarily mean the security will not constitute a floating charge. For example, in *Re Bond Worth Ltd* [1980] Ch 228 it was held that a term in a sale agreement constituted a floating charge notwithstanding that the charge was over existing and not future goods and that the assets comprised in the charge were only likely to change in the sense that they would be sold or used for the purposes of manufacture.

13.3 Circumstances in which a floating charge will crystallise

The time at which a floating charge will crystallise into a fixed equitable charge may be important for the purpose of determining priority. A floating charge will crystallise into a fixed equitable charge on the following events:

- the winding-up of the company;
- the appointment of a receiver;
- the company ceasing to carry on business (*Re Woodroffes (Musical Instruments) Ltd* [1986] Ch 366);
- such other occasions as may be contained in the relevant debenture, for example, failure to repay the loan on demand or notice being given to the company ('automatic crystallisation').

13.4 Priority of charges

In a receivership or liquidation, a floating charge will rank behind the preferential debtors (such as the Inland Revenue, Customs and Excise and employees) for payment (ss 40 and 175 of the Insolvency Act 1986). In contrast, the holder of a fixed charge will be entitled to recover any debt due to him from the secured assets without regard to preferential debts. The insertion of automatic crystallisation clauses in debentures was originally designed to enable floating charges to rank ahead of preferential debts by ensuring that, at the time of receivership or liquidation, the floating charge had been converted into a fixed charge. The Insolvency Act 1986 closed this loophole by defining a floating charge for this purpose as one which, as created, was a floating charge (s 251 of the Insolvency Act). Nevertheless, an automatic crystallisation provision may, in certain circumstances, allow the chargeholder to gain priority over later fixed charges (see below). It should be noted that there are provisions in the Companies Act 1989 concerning charges which will empower the Secretary of State to make regulations requiring particulars to be delivered to Companies House of the circumstances in which crystallisation of a floating charge will occur and, until the appropriate registration is made, any relevant right of crystallisation will not be effective (s 410). It is understood, however, that these amendments are now unlikely to be brought into force in their present form.

Other than as stated above, the Act contains no rules relating to priority. Fixed legal charges and floating charges will, with regard to themselves, rank in the order in which they are created. A floating charge, being an equitable charge, will take subject to a later fixed legal charge unless the charge contains a prohibition on the creation of any prior ranking security (a 'negative pledge' clause) and the legal chargee has notice of this clause. Although particulars of floating charges must be filed at Companies House (see below), there is no space on the relevant form for details of such clauses to be included. Furthermore, *Wilson v Kelland* [1910] 2 Ch 306 held that registration of particulars of a charge constitutes notice of a charge but not of all its detailed provisions which are registered. It is, however, advisable to include a negative pledge clause on the form, since, if a subsequent chargeholder or his solicitor makes a company search, he would have actual knowledge of the clause and would be unable to contend that his charge should take priority through lack of notice.

The rules stated above all assume that the charges have been appropriately registered at Companies House and, if they have not been, any priority they would otherwise have had will be lost.

13.5 Section A: registration of company charges

Certain types of charges are required to be filed on Form 395 within 21 days of their creation. Failure to do so will result in the charge being void against any liquidator, administrator or creditor, although the charge will still be enforceable against the company itself (s 395). The court is able to authorise late filing where the failure to do so was:

> ... accidental, or due to inadvertence or to some other sufficient cause or is not of a nature to prejudice the position of creditors or shareholders of the company, or that on other grounds it is just and equitable to grant relief.

Any rectification of the charges register will be without prejudice to any person who has acquired rights in the intervening period (s 404) and the registration will normally be challengeable by a liquidator if the company goes into liquidation within three months of the making of an order.

Section 396 sets out the charges that are required to be registered:
- a charge for the purpose of securing any issue of debentures;
- a charge on the uncalled share capital of the company;
- a charge created or evidenced by an instrument which, if executed by an individual, would require registration as a bill of sale;
- a charge on land or any interest in it excluding a charge for rent;
- a charge on the book debts of the company;

- a floating charge on the company's undertaking or property;
- a charge on calls made but not paid;
- a charge on a ship or aircraft;
- a charge on goodwill or any intellectual property (as defined).

There is no definition of book debts contained in the Act. Book debts have been judicially construed as debts which would or could be entered in the books of a company in the ordinary course as a debt, even if not so entered (*Independent Automatic Sales Ltd v Knowles & Foster* [1962] 1 WLR 974). *Re Brightlife* held that the credit balance on a company bank account did not fall within 'book and other debts' used in the debenture, since this was not the meaning usually given to the term by businessmen, who would describe it as cash. *Re Charge Card Services Ltd* [1987] Ch 150 went even further and held that it was not conceptually possible for a company to charge in favour of a bank any credit balances on accounts held at that bank. Doubt has been thrown on this decision by the Court of Appeal in *Welsh Development Agency v Export Finance Co Ltd* [1992] BCLC 148, although the case was not overruled. Despite the *Charge Card* decision, the Registrar of Companies has agreed to continue to accept for registration charges over credit balances on the basis that there is some doubt over the correctness of *Charge Card*.

13.5.1 Method of registration

At present, the Act places the duty on the company to deliver particulars of a charge within 21 days of its creation. Particulars can also be delivered by any person who has an interest in the charge and, in practice, it is often the chargeholder or his solicitors who will deal with the appropriate filing, since, if the procedure is not correctly carried out, it is his security that will be prejudiced. Registration is made on Form 395 if the security is a single charge, or on Form 397 if it is one of a series. Form 395 requires the following information to be included:

- date of creation of the charge;
- description of the instrument (if any) creating or evidencing the charge;
- the amount secured by the charge;
- the names and addresses of the persons entitled to the charge;
- short particulars of the property charged.

As mentioned above, 13.4, although there is no space for it, details of any negative pledge clause are often included on the form, usually in the space for short particulars of the property.

The form, together with an original of the relevant debenture, is sent to Companies House. The Registrar will check the terms of the registered particulars against the terms of the charge to ensure accuracy of the particulars. Although 21 days are permitted for registration, it is essential that registration is done at the same time as or as soon as is practical after the execution of the debenture. The Registrar is prepared to permit minor alterations to the filed particulars after the 21 day period (relating to the company name or number or other minor clerical or typing errors), but other changes to the form are not allowed outside the period. Accordingly, if some relevant information is omitted from the particulars, the form will be sent back, for amendment, to the person who submitted it. If the amended form is not received within the 21 day period, the Registrar is unable to accept the particulars for registration without an appropriate order from the court. Therefore, it is essential to submit the particulars at the commencement of the 21 day period in order to maximise the time available for correcting any defect in the particulars.

Once registered, the Registrar will issue a certificate, which is conclusive evidence that all the particulars complied with the requirements of the Act (s 401(2)). Thus, if the register fails to state the amount secured by the charge or the property covered by the charge correctly, this does not affect the rights of the chargeholder, which will be determined by the terms of his charge (*Re C L Nye* [1971] Ch 442).

13.5.2 Charges register

Under the present legislation, the Registrar is required to keep a register of charges in respect of each company, which summarises the terms of the charge, the amount secured, date of creation and registration and identifies the chargeholder. Details of any memorandum of satisfaction and appointment and cessation of receivers are also included (s 401). All limited companies are required to keep at their registered office a register of charges and enter all charges specifically affecting the property of the company and all floating charges. The register is not required to be in any particular form but must give a short description of the property charged, the amount of the charge and name of the chargeholder. The company must also keep a copy of the charge at its registered office (s 407). Both registers are required to be open to inspection by the public.

13.5.3 Release of charge

Once a charge has been released by the chargeholder, the company is able to provide a statutory declaration to the Registrar (Form 403a, or Form 403b if part of the property has been released from the charge or sold) evidencing that fact. The Registrar is then able to place a memorandum of satisfaction on the register of charges of the relevant company.

13.6 Section B: reform

The Companies Act 1989 introduced a number of amendments to the law relating to company charges, but these have not been implemented. This was due to the unpopularity of the proposal to abolish the conclusiveness of the Registrar's certificate (see above, 13.5.1) and the fact that the abolition would cause problems with the Land Registry (which relied on the certificate in preparing its own.)

After an abortive attempt at reform in 1995, the DTI revived the issue of reform of the law relating to the registration of charges in the context of the comprehensive review of company law launched in March 1998 (see below, Chapter 14). A detailed consultation document on the subject was published in October 2000 and is available at the DTI's website (www.dti.gov.uk).

13.7 Receivers

This work does not cover receiverships or administrations, details of which are set out in *Insolvency Law* by Steven Frieze (4th edn, 2001, London: Cavendish Publishing).

14 Company Law Reform

14.1 Introduction

In March 1998, the DTI launched its Company Law Review. This project, managed by an independent Steering Group, is intended to provide a long term fundamental review of core company law with the aim of modernising and simplifying the regulatory framework. The Review is due to end in April 2001, when the Steering Group presents its final report and recommendations to Government.

In March 2000, the Steering Group published *Modern Company Law For a Competitive Economy – Developing the Framework*, a consultation document over 400 pages long, setting out the main areas for review and putting forward a range of specific proposals for reform. These include extensive reform proposals specific to private companies, the most important of which are set out below.

14.2 Private company law reform: proposals

14.2.1 Notice periods

Private companies should be permitted to reduce the period of notice required for shareholder meetings (including the AGM) to 14 calendar days without recourse to the procedures for short notice (see above, Chapter 9).

14.2.2 Written resolutions

The rules governing written resolutions should be relaxed in order to avoid the need for unanimity of votes. There are two suggested methods of achieving this:

(a) allow companies to pass written resolutions by the same majority as would be required to pass the resolution at a meeting of shareholders (that is, simple majority for an ordinary resolution, 75% for a special resolution);

(b) allow companies to pass written resolutions on the basis of a high majority (for example, 90%).

These proposals raise the issue of how that majority would be calculated. One basis could be the relevant majority of those entitled to vote; however, this would be a more demanding test than that for passing a resolution at a meeting (a relevant majority of votes cast). Alternatively, it would also be possible to treat the written resolution as a vote, with shareholders given the opportunity to state in writing whether or not they support the written resolution, the resolution being passed if supported by a relevant majority of votes cast. This could, however, prove complex from an administrative perspective.

It is also proposed to dispense with the requirement to notify the company's auditors (if any) of the content of a written resolution.

14.2.3 Capital maintenance

The Steering Group has produced a number of proposals relating to capital maintenance for private companies:

- Shares with a par value should be abolished; instead, shares would represent a proportion of the value of the company.
- The rules relating to share premium should be replaced with a rule that, when new shares are issued, the undistributable reserves are increased by the net proceeds of the shares.
- The restrictions upon financial assistance by a company for the acquisition of its shares should be relaxed or removed entirely.
- The rules on reduction of share capital should be eased by removing the requirement for court approval, provided that any reduction is supported by a solvency statement.

14.2.4 Authority to allot

The statutory requirement for shareholder authorisation for directors to issue shares should be removed. Instead, allotment would be a matter for directors under their general management powers, unless the company chooses in its articles to restrict directors' powers in some way or to require shareholder approval. It is proposed that this relaxation should be extended to redeemable shares, with directors able to decide the terms of redemption.

14.2.5 Company secretary

The requirement for companies to have a designated company secretary should be lifted. This would not affect a company's obligations to carry out the functions normally carried out by the secretary (record keeping, communications with Companies House, etc), but would allow companies greater flexibility in their administrative arrangements. There is some potential for arguing that larger companies, for whom the administrative burdens are greater, would still require a dedicated secretary; the Steering Group suggests that a threshold based either upon the threshold currently in force for auditors ('small companies' as defined in s 247 need not appoint an auditor where they satisfy two of the following conditions: turnover not more than £2.8 million; a balance sheet total of not more than £1.4 million; 50 or fewer employees), or upon the number of shareholders of the company could be introduced, above which a secretary would be required. If this were to be adopted, it has been suggested that it might be beneficial to introduce a statutory requirement for a secretary of a private company to have the requisite knowledge, experience and qualifications for the post.

14.2.6 Part X of the Companies Act 1985

Part X of the Act, which relates to the enforcement of fair dealing by directors, should be modified for private companies, to allow transactions of the company requiring shareholder approval to be approved by a written resolution (following the procedure outlined above, 14.2.2). It is also proposed that the requirement for a sole director to disclose interests in contracts to the board be replaced with an obligation either to record such an interest in writing or to disclose the interest to the shareholders.

14.2.7 Arbitration in shareholder disputes

The disproportionate costs, both in terms of money and time, which shareholder actions, particularly under s 459, can impose upon private companies, has prompted the Steering Group to recommend the introduction of an option for arbitration in such disputes. This could take the form of a requirement on courts considering a s 459 or a derivative action to adjourn in order to facilitate (though not to impose) arbitration between the company and its shareholders, unless there is a good reason not to do so. This could potentially be strengthened by a statutory presumption in favour of arbitration and/or costs sanctions for a party who unreasonably refuses arbitration.

14.2.8 Model constitution

The Steering Group has recommended the development of a model constitution for private companies to replace the memorandum and articles. This would be a modern and 'user-friendly' replacement for Table A, more closely tailored to the requirements and concerns of private companies. It would operate as a neutral, workable set of default rules, which companies could choose to amend or exclude at will. Any matter of sufficient importance to be applied universally should be provided for by statute, not in the model constitution.

Some of the specific ways in which the model constitution would differ from Table A are as follows:

- the regulations relating to liens and calls on shares and forfeiture would be removed, as they are rarely required by private companies;
- the requirement for directors to retire by rotation would also be removed, as it is inappropriate for most private companies;
- amendments would also be required to reflect the reform proposals detailed above.

14.2.9 Actions by minority shareholders

The Steering Group, on the recommendation of the Law Commission, has put forward a proposal to replace the exceptions to the rule in *Foss v Harbottle* (see the discussion above, 12.1) with a statutory code, which would set out the circumstances in which a derivative action would be permissible.

14.2.10 Companies House filing reforms

Over the last couple of years, a number of changes have been introduced to the requirements for filing information at Companies House. The effect of the changes has been twofold. First, new forms under ss 287 and 288 of the Act have been introduced to enable the Registrar of Companies to use Intelligent Character Recognition technology (ICR) (Companies (Forms) (Amendment) Regulations 1998 (SI 1998/1702)). This change reflects the shift in market practice away from document-based filing to filing by electronic means.

Secondly, both the layout and information to be disclosed on a number of forms has been altered. The alterations include:

- A reorganisation of the layout of the share allotment details section on Form 88(2) (Companies (Forms) (Amendment) Regulations 1999 (SI 1999/2356)).
- A clarification on Form 88(2) of the circumstances in which details must be given of the allotment of shares which are allotted as fully or partly paid up otherwise than in cash (Companies (Forms) (Amendment) (No 2) Regulations 1999 (SI 1999/2678)).
- Form 288b no longer requires a reason for the termination of the director's appointment to be disclosed. It has been reworded to make it clear that an appointment can be terminated by means other than by resignation (Companies (Forms) (Amendment) Regulations 1999 (SI 1999/2356));
- Forms 363a and 363s (prescribed for the purposes of s 363(2) of the Act) have been amended in the following way:
  - private companies no longer have to state whether resolutions are in force to dispense with the need to lay accounts and reports before the company at the general meeting and to dispense with the holding of AGMs;
  - companies no longer have to disclose the other directorships and former names of individual directors; and
  - companies no longer have to disclose the other directorships of corporate directors (Companies (Contents of Annual Return) Regulations 1999 (SI 1999/2322); Companies (Forms) (Amendment) Regulations 1999 (SI 1998/2356)).

The overall effect has been to reduce the burden of disclosure on companies submitting information to Companies House. Although this arguably reduces the amount of information available to shareholders and the general public through Companies House, these changes are thought to be beneficial, as they streamline the system and are consistent with the general trend towards electronic filing.

15 Forms

Package: 'Laserform'
by Laserform International Ltd.

*Please complete in typescript,
or in bold black capitals.*

CHFP025

Notes on completion appear on final page

10

First directors and secretary and intended situation of registered office

Company Name in full | Licence to Kill Limited

Proposed Registered Office | 3, Casino Avenue
(PO Box numbers only, are not acceptable)

Post town | Ealing

County / Region | Greater London | Postcode | W5 5DS

If the memorandum is delivered by an agent for the subscriber(s) of the memorandum mark the box opposite and give the agent's name and address.

X

Agent's Name | Goldfinger, Blofelt & Co.

Address | 1, Lucre Street

Hampleton

Post town | Winchester

County / Region | Hampshire | Postcode | WI5 2Q7

Number of continuation sheets attached | 0

Please give the name, address, telephone number and, if available, a DX number and Exchange of the person Companies House should contact if there is any query.

Goldfinger, Blofelt & Co.
1 Lucre Street
Hampleton

Tel Your Tel No.01958 652641
DX numberDX: 300 DX exchange Exchange

Companies House receipt date barcode

When you have completed and signed the form please send it to the Registrar of Companies at:
Companies House, Crown Way, Cardiff, CF14 3UZ   DX 33050 Cardiff
for companies registered in England and Wales
or
Companies House, 37 Castle Terrace, Edinburgh, EH1 2EB
for companies registered in Scotland   **DX 235 Edinburgh**

Laserform International 12/99

Company Secretary (see notes 1 5)

Company name	Licence to Kill Limited

NAME *Style / Title: Miss

*Honours etc:

* Voluntary details

Forename(s): Annabel Margaret

Surname: Moneypenny

Previous forename(s):

Previous surname(s):

Address
Usual residential address
For a corporation, give the registered or principal office address.

Primrose Cottage, Primrose Drive

Denham

Post town: Uxbridge

County / Region: Middlesex   Postcode: UB9 5DE

Country: England

I consent to act as secretary of the company named on page 1

Consent signature   **Date**

Directors (see notes 1 5)

Please list directors in alphabetical order

NAME *Style / Title: Commander   *Honours etc:

Forename(s): James Robert

Surname: Bond

Previous forename(s):

Previous surname(s):

Address
Usual residential address
For a corporation, give the registered or principal office address.

12, Martini Mews

Post town: Hampstead

County / Region: Greater London   Postcode: NW11 MI5

Country: England

	Day	Month	Year		
Date of birth	0 7	0 4	6 0	**Nationality**	British

Business occupation: Civil Servant

Other directorships: "Q" Ventures Limited

Stunts Limited

I consent to act as director of the company named on page 1

Consent signature   **Date**

Directors (continued) (see notes 1-5)

NAME *Style / Title	Mrs
*Honours etc	
Forename(s)	Rose
Surname	Klebb
Previous forename(s)	–
Previous surname(s)	Antov
Address	The Old Forge, Blacksmith Road
Usual residential address. For a corporation, give the registered or principal office address.	Little Anvil
Post town	Southampton
County / Region	Hampshire
Postcode	SO4 290
Country	England
Date of birth	Day 27 Month 07 Year 61
Nationality	Russian
Business occupation	Diplomat
Other directorships	None

* Voluntary details

I consent to act as director of the company named on page 1

Consent signature _____ **Date** _____

This section must be signed by

Either

an agent on behalf of all subscribers   Signed _____ Date _____

Or the subscribers   Signed _____ Date _____

(i.e those who signed as members on the memorandum of association).

Signed _____ Date _____

Signed _____ Date _____

Signed _____ Date _____

Signed _____ Date _____

Notes

1. Show for an individual the full forename(s) NOT INITIALS and surname together with any previous forename(s) or surname(s).

   If the director or secretary is a corporation or Scottish firm - show the corporate or firm name on the surname line.

   Give previous forename(s) or surname(s) except that:

   - for a married woman, the name by which she was known before marriage need not be given;

   - names not used since the age of 18 or for at least 20 years need not be given.

   A peer, or an individual known by a title, may state the title instead of or in addition to the forename(s) and surname and need not give the name by which that person was known before he or she adopted the title or succeeded to it.

   Address:

   Give the usual residential address.

   In the case of a corporation or Scottish firm give the registered or principal office.

   Subscribers:

   The form must be signed personally either by the subscriber(s) or by a person or persons authorised to sign on behalf of the subscriber(s).

2. Directors known by another description:

   - A director includes any person who occupies that position even if called by a different name, for example, governor, member of council.

3. Directors details:

   - Show for each individual director the director's date of birth, business occupation and nationality.
   The date of birth must be given for every individual director.

4. Other directorships:

   - Give the name of every company of which the person concerned is a director or has been a director at any time in the past 5 years. You may exclude a company which either **is** or at **all times during the past 5 years,** when the person was a director, **was**:

   - dormant,

   - a parent company which wholly owned the company making the return,

   - a wholly owned subsidiary of the company making the return, or

   - another wholly owned subsidiary of the same parent company.

   If there is insufficient space on the form for other directorships you may use a separate sheet of paper, which should include the company's number and the full name of the director.

5. Use Form 10 continuation sheets or photocopies of page 2 to provide details of joint secretaries or additional directors.

12

Package:	'Laserform'
by Laserform International Ltd.	

Please complete in typescript, or in bold black capitals.

CHFP025

Declaration on application for registration

Company Name in full Licence to Kill Limited

I, William Goldfinger

of 1, Lucre Street, Hampleton, Winchester, Hampshire

do solemnly and sincerely declare that I am a [Solicitor engaged in the formation of the company] [person named as director or secretary of the company in the statement delivered to the Registrar under section 10 of the Companies Act 1985] † and that all the requirements of the Companies Act 1985 in respect of the registration of the above company and of matters precedent and incidental to it have been complied with.

And I make this solemn Declaration conscientiously believing the same to be true and by virtue of the Statutory Declarations Act 1835.

† Please delete as appropriate.

Declarant's signature

Declared at 3, Lucre Street, Hampleton, Winchester, Hampshire

	Day	Month	Year
On	2 2	0 4	2 0 0 0

● Please print name.

before me ● Hugo Drax

Signed   **Date** 22/04/2000

†A Commissioner for Oaths or Notary Public or Justice of the Peace or Solicitor

Please give the name, address, telephone number and, if available, a DX number and Exchange of the person Companies House should contact if there is any query.

Goldfinger, Blofelt & Co.
1, Lucre Street, Hampleton, Winchester, Hampshire

Tel 01958 652 641
DX number DX: 300   DX exchange Exchange

Companies House receipt date barcode

When you have completed and signed the form please send it to the Registrar of Companies at:
Companies House, Crown Way, Cardiff, CF14 3UZ   DX 33050 Cardiff
for companies registered in England and Wales
or
Companies House, 37 Castle Terrace, Edinburgh, EH1 2EB
for companies registered in Scotland   **DX 235 Edinburgh**

Laserform International 12/99

Package: 'Laserform'
by Laserform International Ltd.

Please complete in typescript, or in bold black capitals.

CHFP025

88(2)
Return of Allotment of Shares

Company Number   007

Company name in full   Licence to Kill Limited

Shares allotted (including bonus shares):

	From			To		
Date or period during which shares were allotted *(If shares were allotted on one date enter that date in the "from" box)*	Day	Month	Year	Day	Month	Year
	0 1	0 5	2 0 0 0			

Class of shares *(ordinary or preference etc)*	Ordinary	
Number allotted	1,000	
Nominal value of each share	£1	
Amount (if any) paid or due on each share *(including any share premium)*	£2	

List the names and addresses of the allottees and the number of shares allotted to each overleaf

If the allotted shares are fully or party paid up otherwise than in cash please state:

% that each share is to be treated as paid up	
Consideration for which the shares were allotted *(This information must be supported by the duly stamped contract or by the duly stamped particulars on Form 88(3) if the contract is not in writing)*	

Companies House receipt date barcode

When you have completed and signed the form please send it to the Registrar of Companies at:

Companies House, Crown Way, Cardiff, CF14 3UZ   DX 33050 Cardiff
For companies registered in England and Wales

Companies House, 37 Castle Terrace, Edinburgh, EH1 2EB
For companies registered in Scotland   DX 235 Edinburgh

Names and addresses of the allottees *(List joint share allotments consecutively)*

Shareholder details	Shares and share class allotted	
Name James Robert Bond	Class of shares allotted	Number allotted
Address 12, Martini Mews, Hampstead, London	Ordinary	900
UK Postcode N W 1 1 M I 5		
Name Marianne Clara Moneypenny	Class of shares allotted	Number allotted
Address Primrose Cottage, Primrose Drive, Denham, Uxbridge, Middlesex	Ordinary	100
UK Postcode U B 9 5 D E		
Name	Class of shares allotted	Number allotted
Address		
UK Postcode		
Name	Class of shares allotted	Number allotted
Address		
UK Postcode		
Name	Class of shares allotted	Number allotted
Address		
UK Postcode		

Please enter the number of continuation sheets (if any) attached to this form   **0**

Signed _____   **Date** 01/05/2000

A director / ~~Secretary~~ / ~~Administrator~~ / ~~Administrative receiver~~ / ~~Receiver manager~~ / ~~Receiver~~   *Please delete as appropriate*

Please give the name, address, telephone number and, if available, a DX number and Exchange of the person Companies House should contact if there is any query.

Goldfinger, Blofelt & Co.

1, Lucre Street, Hampleton, Winchester, Hampshire

WI5 2Q7   Tel 01958 652 641

DX number 300   DX exchange

G

CHFP025

COMPANIES FORM No. 123

Notice of increase in nominal capital

123

Please do not write in this margin

Pursuant to section 123 of the Companies Act 1985

Please complete legibly, preferably in black type, or bold block lettering

To the Registrar of Companies
(Address overleaf)

For official use

Company number
 007

Name of company

* insert full name of company

* Licence to Kill Limited

gives notice in accordance with section 123 of the above Act that by resolution of the company dated 2 May 2000 the nominal capital of the company has been increased by £ 1,000 beyond the registered capital of £ 1,000 .

† the copy must be printed or in some other form aproved by the registrar

A copy of the resolution authorising the increase is attached. †

The conditions (eg. voting rights, dividend rights, winding-up rights etc.) subject to which the new shares have been or are to be issued are as follows :

The new ordinary shares rank pari passu in all respects with the existing ordinary shares

Please tick here if continued overleaf

‡ Insert Director, Secretary, Administrator, Administrative Receiver or Receiver (Scotland) as appropriate

Signed   Designation ‡ Director   Date 02/05/00

Presentor's name address and reference (if any) :

Goldfinger, Blofelt & Co.
1, Lucre Street
Hampleton
Winchester
Hampshire

For official Use
General Section

Post room

Laserform International 12/99

Notes

The address for companies registered in England and Wales or Wales is:-

The Registrar of Companies
Companies House
Crown Way
Cardiff
CF14 3UZ

or, for companies registered in Scotland:-

The Registrar of Companies
Companies House
37 Castle Terrace
Edinburgh
EH1 2EB

Package: 'Laserform'
by Laserform International Ltd.

Please complete in typescript,
or in bold black capitals.

CHFP025

Change of accounting reference date

225

Company Number 007

Company Name in Full Licence to Kill Limited

The accounting reference period ending — Day 3 1 | Month 1 2 | Year 2 0 0 0

is shortened/extended† so as to end on — Day 3 1 | Month 0 3 | Year 2 0 0 1

NOTES

You may use this form to change the accounting date relating to either the current or the immediately previous accounting period.

a. You **may not** change a period for which the accounts are already overdue.

b. You **may not** extend a period beyond 18 months unless the company is subject to an administration order.

c. You **may not** extend periods more than once in five years unless:

 1. the company is subject to an administration order, or

 2. you have the specific approval of the Secretary of State, (please enclose a copy), or

 3. you are extending the company's accounting reference period to align with that of a parent or subsidiary undertaking established in the European Economic Area, or

 4. the form is being submitted by an overseas company.

Subsequent periods will end on the same day and month in future years.

If extending more than once in five years, please indicate in the box the number of the provision listed in note c. on which you are relying.

Signed

Date 01/05/2000

† Please delete as appropriate

† a director / xxxxxx /xxxxxxx xxxxxxxxx xxxxxx /xxxxxxx xxxxxxxxx / xxxxxxxxxxxxx /xxxxxxxxxxxxx xx xxxxx xxxxx xxxxxxxxx x

Please give the name, address, telephone number, and if available, a DX number and Exchange, for the person Companies House should contact if there is any query

Goldfinger, Blofelt & Co.
1. Lucre Street, Hampleton, Winchester, Hampshire, WI5 2Q7

Tel 01958 652 641
DX number DX: 300   DX exchange Exchange

Companies House receipt date barcode

When you have completed and signed the form please send it to the Registrar of Companies at:
Companies House, Crown Way, Cardiff, CF14 3UZ   DX 33050 Cardiff
for companies registered in England and Wales
or
Companies House, 37 Castle Terrace, Edinburgh, EH1 2EB
for companies registered in Scotland   DX 235 Edinburgh

Laserform International 12/99

288b

Terminating appointment as director or secretary
(NOT for appointment (use Form 288a) or change of particulars (use Form 288c))

Package: 'Laserform' by Laserform International Ltd.

Please complete in typescript, or in bold black capitals.

CHFP025

Company Number: 007

Company Name in full: Licence to Kill Limited

Date of termination of appointment: Day 22 Month 09 Year 2000

as director: X   as secretary:

Please mark the appropriate box. If terminating appointment as a director and secretary mark both boxes.

NAME — Please insert details as previously notified to Companies House.

*Style / Title: Mrs
*Honours etc:
Forename(s): Rosa
Surname: Klebb

†**Date of Birth:** Day 22 Month 07 Year 61

A serving director, secretary etc must sign the form below.

Signed: **Date:** 22/09/2000

(** serving director/~~secretary/administrator/administrative receiver/receiver manager/receiver~~)

* Voluntary details.
† Directors only.
** Please delete as appropriate

Please give the name, address, telephone number and, if available, a DX number and Exchange of the person Companies House should contact if there is any query.

Goldfinger, Blofelt & Co.
1, Lucre Street, Hampleton, Winchester, Hampshire, WI5 2Q7

Tel 01958 652 641
DX number DX: 300   DX exchange Exchange

When you have completed and signed the form please send it to the Registrar of Companies at:
Companies House, Crown Way, Cardiff, CF14 3UZ   DX 33050 Cardiff
for companies registered in England and Wales
or
Companies House, 37 Castle Terrace, Edinburgh, EH1 2EB
for companies registered in Scotland   DX 235 Edinburgh

Companies House receipt date barcode

Laserform International 12/99

16 Useful Addresses

Companies House

From 2 April 2001, Companies House has a new national telephone number for all enquiries: 0870 333 3636. The web address for Companies House is www.companies-house.gov.uk. Regional offices are listed below.

Cardiff

Companies House
Crown Way
Cardiff CF4 3UZ

Tel: 02920 388 588
Fax: 02920 380 900
General Enquiries: 02920 380 801
Opening hours: 9 am to 5 pm

Postal and fax searches:

Tel: 02920 380 819
Fax: 02920 380 517

London

Companies House
21 Bloomsbury Square
London WC1B 3XD

Tel: 02920 380 801
Fax: 02920 380 900
Opening hours: 9 am to 5 pm

Edinburgh

Companies House
37 Castle Terrace
Edinburgh EH1 2EB

Tel: 0131 535 5800
Fax: 0131 535 5820
General Enquiries: 0131 535 5800
Opening Hours: 9 am to 5 pm

Postal and fax services:

Tel: 0131 535 5868
Fax: 0131 535 5820

Leeds

Companies House
25 Queen Street
Leeds LS1 2TW

Tel: 01132 338 338
Fax: 01132 338 335
Opening hours: 9 am to 4 pm

Birmingham

Companies House
Central Library
Chamberlain Square
Birmingham B3 3HQ

Tel: 0121 233 9047
Fax: 0121 233 9052
Opening hours: 9 am to 4 pm

Manchester

Companies House
75 Mosely Street
Manchester M2 2HR

Tel: 0161 236 7500
Fax: 0161 237 5258
Opening hours: 9 am to 4 pm

Glasgow

Companies House
7 West George Street
Glasgow G2 1BQ

Tel: 0141 221 5513
Fax: 0141 225 2870
Opening hours: 9 am to 5 pm

17 Time Periods and Penalties

Matter to be registered	Time period for registration and form to be completed	Maximum penalty	Daily default fine for failure to complete
Allotment of shares	Within one month of allotment file Form 88(2) or Form 88(3) where details of the contract pursuant to which the shares were allotted is not reduced to writing	'£5,000 (summary prosecution). No maximum (indictment)'	£500
Annual return	Within 28 days of the first anniversary of incorporation or the date on which the last return was made up on Form 363	'£5,000'	£500
Audited accounts	Ten months after the end of the relevant accounting reference date	—	—

Audited accounts	Ten months after the end of the relevant accounting reference date	'£5,000. In addition civil damages are payable under s 242A as follows: • up to 3 months late £100 • up to 6 months late £250 • up to 12 months late £500 • more than 12 months late £1,000'	____
Change to accounting reference date	File Form 225 in order to effect alteration	____	____
Change in directors or secretary	Within 14 days of the appointment or removal on Form 288	'£5,000'	'£1,000'
Change in registered office	Change only take effect 14 days after Form 287 lodged	____	____
Change to memorandum or articles of association	Special resolution to be filed within 15 days together with a print of the memorandum and articles as amended (s 18)	'£1,000'	£500

'Consolidation, division, subdivision, redemption or cancellation of shares'	File Form 122 within one month of the relevant alteration to the share capital'	'£1,000'	£100
Creation of charge	File Form 395 within 21 days of the creation of the charge	'£5,000 (summary). No maximum (indictment) – see *note (1)*'	£500
Increase share capital	Ordinary resolution to be filed within 15 days together with Form 123 summarising the rights attaching to the new shares	'£1,000'	£100
Purchase of own shares by a company	File Form 169 within 278 days of purchase	'£5,000 (summary) No maximum (indictment)'	£500
Release of a charge	File Form 403a	___	___
Resolutions to be filed in accordance with s 380 (see 4.3)	File resolution – signed by chairman of meeting within 15 days of its being passed	'£1,000'	£100
Removal of auditor before the expiration of his term of office	File Form 391 within 14 days of the passing of the relevant resolution	'£1,000'	£100

Note (1) – Charge is void against any liquidator, administrator or creditor and the money secured by the charge becomes immediately payable.

18 Further Reading

18.1 Looseleaf works

Boyle, AJ (ed), *Gore-Browne on Companies*, 44th edn, 1998, London: Jordan

Morse, G (ed), *Charlesworth and Morse: Company Law*, 16th edn, 1999, London: Sweet & Maxwell

18.2 Books and official reports

Pettet, BG and Prentice, DD (eds), *Gower's Principles of Modern Company Law*, 6th edn, 1997, London: Sweet & Maxwell

Department of Trade and Industry, *Modern Company Law For a Competitive Economy – Developing the Framework*, 2000, London: HMSO

Farrar, JF, *Farrar's Company Law*, 4th edn, 1998, London: Butterworths

Mayson, S, French, D and Ryan, C, *Mayson, French & Ryan on Company Law*, 15th edn, 1998, London: Blackstone

Stamp, M, *Practical Company Law*, 2nd edn, 1996, London: Sweet & Maxwell

Wareham, R (ed), *Tolley's Company Law Handbook 2000–2001*, 2000, Croydon: Tolley

18.3 Journals

Business Law Review, The Hague: Kluwer

Company Lawyer, London: Sweet & Maxwell

Journal of Business Law, London: Sweet & Maxwell

New Law Journal, London: Butterworths

PLC (Practical Law for Companies), London: Legal and Commercial Publishing

Solicitors Journal, London: Sweet & Maxwell